The Game That Never Happened

Ian Syson

# The Game That Never Happened

The Vanishing History of Soccer in Australia

Ian Syson

Sports and Editorial Services Australia

Published by Sports and Editorial Services Australia, 9 Knowles Court, Bannockburn, Victoria 3331, www.sesasport.com.au

First published 2018

Distributed by Dennis Jones and Associates, Unit 1/10 Melrich Road, Bayswater, Victoria 3153

Copyright © Ian Syson 2018

Editing and proofreading by Frances Hay

Cover design and layout by Vulgar Enterprises of North Carlton

Printed by Geelong Print Solutions Pty Ltd, 5 Sandtoft Court, Highton, Victoria 3216

Cataloguing-in-publication data is available from the National Library of Australia.

ISBN: 978-0-9946019-3-3

Set in 11.5/14 Garamond

Cover photograph: 'Soccer Silhouettes' taken from the *Argus*, 9 August 1929, 5.

*for Dan and Harry*

# CONTENTS

# ACKNOWLEDGEMENTS

As is the case with all books, this one is a collection and curation of ideas and inspirations. While I'd like to thank all the individuals and institutions involved I am bound to miss a few; so apologies in advance.

A circle of people around me whom I count as both friends and colleagues have had tremendous influence on my thinking during the production of the book. Their traces are laced throughout its pages. Australia's foremost soccer historian, Roy Hay, has encouraged, cajoled and criticised me in equal measure for nearly ten years now. He and Frances Hay have my gratitude for deciding to publish *The Game That Never Happened*. Frances is a fine editor and she has done a great job in shaping the ends that I had roughly hewn. Paul Mavroudis has been a constant inspiration-cum-irritation throughout and has settled me down and lifted me up when appropriate – and sometimes when it wasn't. Athas Zafiris and Joe Gorman have left their marks as well, in their friendship, and in their research assistance and structural editing respectively. Anita Milicevic probably saved the book from being cast away with a timely, serendipitous intervention. Paul Conroy influenced the founding ideas of the book with a series of debates and arguments that left us drained but wiser. Other significant sounding boards have been, in no particular order, Damian Smith, James Hothersall, Mark Boric, Maggie Koumi, Walter Pless, Chris Egan, Dermot Clancy, Anthony Colangelo, Les Street, Bonita Mersiades, Ben Goldsmith, Brogan Renshaw, Phil Dimitriadis, Greg Downes, Adam Muyt, Ted Smith, Trevor Ruddell, Bill Murray, Phil Mosely, Matthew Klugmann, Mal Neil, Andrew Howe, George Kaye (among many in Clarendon Corner), the Football Federation Victoria History Committee and members of the soccerati section of

#SokkahTwitter (you know who you are). Jason Steger, literary editor of the *Age*, is fundamentally responsible for this book even existing. He encouraged me to write about the game by tossing soccer book after soccer book in my direction to review. It diverted me from my literary research and whetted an appetite that apparently can't be satisfied.

A number of individuals also contributed to the book on a professional basis. Melissa Walsh, Chris Riordan and Claire Royall all proved to be excellent research assistants who provided important sets of sources for me to use. Several journalists have been particularly supportive: Andy Harper and Simon Hill are two of the more prominent ones, but many others, working as they do in a culture that doesn't really want them, have been strong and steady beacons.

I interviewed a number of people earlier this decade who provided leads and ideas that were vital in the book's development. Hugh 'Shuggy' Murney, Ted Smith, Betty Hoar, Don Di Fabrizio and the late Fred Villiers and Hammy McMeechan, among others, were sources of wonderful stories. The Epilogue – which was originally published in *Neos Kosmos* and *Meanjin* and in which I hit upon the phrase, 'the game that never happened' – would not have been written without Hugh and Hammy's help and inspiration.

I need also to thank my employer, Victoria University, for support over many years. A number of deans, especially Bronwyn Cran, showed great faith in my research, despite the extent to which it diverged from my day job teaching literature, and provided research time and some funding. Football Federation Victoria and Football Federation Tasmania gave me opportunities and spaces to work in practical soccer environments that provided a great boost for my research. In recent times Northern New South Wales Football has stepped up in important ways, providing great financial support for my next project (already underway) on the Soccer Anzacs of the Newcastle region. In doing so they provided incidental moral support that helped me get over the line with *The Game That Never Happened*.

The tremendous collections at the National Library of Australia, the State Library of Victoria and the Melbourne Cricket Club Library were fantastic foundations for my research. The book would simply not have been possible without the NLA's Trove collection of digitised newspapers and photographs.

A good portion of the book has been published in article or essay form in *Neos Kosmos*, *Meanjin*, *The International Journal of the History of Sport*, *Sporting Traditions*, *Leopold Method*, *Soccer & Society*, *Shoot Farken*, the *Conversation*, the *Footy Almanac* and the *Football Record*. The editorial process at a number of these journals and magazines provided valuable input that improved the quality of my work.

Many workmates have given generous if baffled support: 'Why are you writing about football codes when you teach literature?' Of these, my friend and colleague John Weldon has been a constant in my process of research and writing. Any number of times I have burst into his office announcing one more juicy morsel of soccer trivia gleaned from Trove. I thank him for his friendship and for always responding with the bemused forbearance of a parent happy that their child has at last found an interest that will keep them off the streets.

Finally, my family gave me years of support during the long process of writing this book and I will be ever grateful. On the cricket and soccer fields, and futsal courts, my boys gave me much joy and inspiration. May they continue to do so.

# INTRODUCTION

Soccer in Australia has contended with dogs, demons and destabilisers since the first spherical balls rolled off the ships in the 1830s. The game's legitimacy has been questioned from the outside ever since it was first advocated in the 1860s and while its first fleeting steps of organisation were taken in the 1870s.[1] Dozens of reasons – including the game's putative foreignness, feebleness, degenerate participants, absence of masculinity, wealth, corruption, colonialism and imperialism – have been used to cast doubt upon soccer's right to exist on this continent.

As a result the quality of belonging felt by many of the game's adherents has been diminished in most places in Australia for most of that history.[2] A sense of inclusion and the possession of 'terrains of commonality', established clubhouses, long tenancy of enclosed playing spaces and entrenched media channels have too rarely been felt and held by soccer in Australia.[3] A kind of embarrassment or even shame is often attached to a commitment to the game. To be a soccer player, supporter or advocate is to adopt an uncanny position in relation to many perceptions of Australian mainstream culture.

There are four main football codes in Australia. While each has a presence in each state, Association football (soccer) has the broadest national coverage and the highest participation figures. While soccer has some local strongholds, it is almost universally the second football code in each state or locality in terms of revenue and interest. Rugby League dominates in the more heavily populated northern states of the eastern seaboard and Australian Rules is the main code in the rest of the nation, with its origins and historical epicentre in Melbourne. This division is sometimes referred to as the Barassi Line, coined by Melbourne historian Ian Turner and named after the father of a famous Australian Rules player.[4] Rugby Union is presently in League's shadow in the northern states, though it is often enjoyed at the private-school level throughout the country. Since 1880, this patchwork has been ever changing. Its seams and tears are indices of the conflict between and within codes for much of the games' histories in Australia.

Negative perceptions of soccer relate strongly to memory. The game has been present at key moments in Australian history yet the broader culture and soccer itself simply do not remember. Reactivating memory is a key to the solution of soccer's problems of historiographical invisibility.

This reactivation is not an easy process, even on a sheer practical level. While the recent digitisation of Australian newspaper archives has made this task somewhat easier than it used to be, a nonetheless significant amount of trawling for previously ignored counter-narratives has been performed in the research for the book.[5]

But the difficulties are more than practical. 'History-making, or the construction of views of the past in any society, is the product of a struggle of a particular interpretation of that event or period,' wrote the historian Lynn Abrams.

> And when a hegemonic view emerges it generally excludes or mutes alternative or counter interpretations. Those who hold alternative interpretations have difficulty narrating or expressing their memories because they cannot fit them into the dominant narrative, the collective memory.[6]

The telling of this story is inevitably a political task, a reactivation of memory that will challenge and upset dominant narratives and those who hold them dear.

Organised soccer is over 130 years old in Australia. At the time of publication, well over 500,000 adult Australians participate in organised outdoor soccer competitions, higher participation levels than any other team sport.[7] At its elite level, soccer is capable of generating massive television viewing statistics. A Socceroos game at the World Cup, for example, is one of the high-water marks in Australian televised sports viewing. While soccer tends only to be the second football code wherever it is played in Australia, it nonetheless has the kind of demographic coverage that the other football codes envy. Soccer's numerical strengths are indicated by its status as the 'go to' game for Australia-wide advertising narratives that represent children at energetic play.

One long-standing frustration for the proponents of soccer in Australia is that many of these tens of thousands of juniors end up playing and supporting other codes of football at the senior level. This drift may well be the game's fundamental problem as it tries to establish itself on a stable footing in Australian sporting life.[8] At the elite level, Australian Rules footballers such as Peter McKenna, Adam Goodes and Peter Matera were good junior soccer players.[9] From Rugby League, Andrew Johns starred with the round ball as a junior in Newcastle. Preston Campbell loved playing soccer as a boy but left the game to follow his good friend Nathan Blacklock to Rugby League.[10] Each of these sportsmen made the switch in their teens. This is a trend that leaves many soccer supporters wondering if their game might have had more success had those players and others stayed in the game. The words, 'He would have been a great soccer player!' have often passed their lips.

So this game, even with such apparent comparative advantages, has fared badly in Australia. Since the 1860s, organised soccer has sought a place in Australian society only to be rebuffed and rejected as a foreign or even alien game, a threat, sometimes even a menace to Australian masculinity and life in general.[11] The game has endured sustained media myopia offset by frequent outbursts of intense and spiteful attention. Legendary player Johnny Warren encapsulated this anti-soccer mentality in the title of his memoir, *Sheilas, Wogs and Poofters*.

While Warren's title doesn't quite represent either the totality or the subtlety of opposition, it does capture the vituperation and the spirit of a different age. He relates the 'daunting image' of a tickertape parade for the Socceroos in Sydney in 1969 in the context of an otherwise positive welcome home:

> I had taken my allocated place in one of the sports cars
> which had been organised for the event. The cavalcade was
> snaking its way through the streets and turned a corner. This
> one particular corner, like so many of its kind in Sydney,
> was adorned by a pub. Wooing the punters to drink from

its kegs were pictures on its outer wall of rugby, cricket and horse racing. True-blue Aussie sports. Spilling out of the pub's doors were tank-topped, steel-cap-booted, tattooed workers quenching their thirst after the dust of the day's work. 'Fuckin' poofters,' some hooted at us. 'Dago bastards,' followed others. The odd projectile was hurled our way. Needless to say, I had, in my life, felt much safer than I did during that parade.[12]

The recent relative successes of soccer in Australia might tend to suggest that the bigoted attitude that confronted Warren is a thing of the past. The way that the A-League and well-attended international fixtures have elbowed themselves some room in the mainstream of Australian sports media indicates a new-found respect for the game has been established in Australia. However, the battle may not be over. Even when the vulgar and coarse resentment is peeled away a core of repulsion, sometimes principled, more often irrational, remains.

The former comes from a writer like Martin Flanagan who believes that any weakening of Australian Rules football because of soccer's rise will damage local culture, already embattled by the manifold forces of globalisation:

> Our Game has a unique place, not only in Australian
> sport, but in Australian culture which, in my experience,
> is obvious to outsiders. I can admire the Australian rugby
> union team and enjoy watching them play, but at the end
> of the day it is a British game they're playing. Australian
> football is a marvellous sporting invention that found its
> way into the hearts of people and infiltrated other aspects of
> their lives so that it became something by which you knew
> families and suburbs and towns and, more recently with the
> national competition, different parts of Australia.[13]

This argument is flawed in relation to Sydney and broad regions of the two northern states of New South Wales and Queensland, something that Flanagan tacitly admits with his vague use of 'different parts of Australia'. The problem is that Australian Rules is an irrelevance for many Australians, even many of those who are interested in sport. They do not play it; they do not watch it; they fail to understand it. Some hate it. Nor have they experienced the purported social benefits of the game to which Flanagan refers. Significantly, in one of the heartlands of Australian mythology, what might be called the Waltzing Matilda country of outback Queensland, Australian Rules was until recently an utterly foreign game and did not belong. Flanagan is guilty of making a national generalisation out of a regional truth.

In many regions and towns soccer has a continuous history of more than 100 years where the game has been, for generations of Australians and waves of migrants, an important pillar of their communities. In Flanagan's home state of Tasmania, the South Hobart Football Club has been in existence for more than 100 years and has played at the same home ground for almost all of that time. The club belongs in and to the community in ways that Flanagan would admire in relation to an Australian Rules club.

Representing a very different perspective is a writer like Michael Duffy, whose article, 'Jig is up – give World Cup the boot', published shortly after Australia's good performance in the 2006 World Cup, is a checklist of predictable prejudice that masks his own failure to understand the game. It's boring; not enough scoring; should be allowed to use hands; too much play-acting, in his opinion. He talks about an experience of watching the World Cup that, given his attitudes and the second-person persona adopted, is probably either second-hand or made up:

> You rose from your bed in the early hours to spend an
> hour and a half watching the ball move from one player
> to another several hundred times without passing through
> the white posts at either end of the field more than once or
> twice. It was like golf without the excitement.[14]

If Flanagan adopts a Left-nationalist position in worrying about soccer's globalising effects, Duffy comes from the free-market Right and argues the very opposite. Inspired by the American academic economist Allen Sanderson, Duffy suggests that Australians are very much like Americans and their resistance to soccer should be seen as exemplary. He cites Sanderson who believes that those Americans who support soccer 'are uncomfortable with competitions that produce winners and losers, and soccer appeals to their egalitarian, risk-averse streak. The same crowd usually also can be counted on to oppose globalisation.'[15]

Duffy also believes soccer is a force of political correctness. 'Lots of parents force their children to play football for reasons of social engineering,' he wrote, 'they want to make their boys more like girls and their girls more like boys.'[16] For Duffy, men's sport is about upper body strength. As a sport that disallows the use of hands, soccer therefore runs against the spirit of unfettered competition that characterises the true sporting contest.

Despite their cultural and political differences, Flanagan and Duffy end up on the same side in this argument. This speaks greatly of the general antipathy to soccer in Australia, particularly from middle-aged men with positions of some cultural influence. Yet Duffy and Flanagan did not invent their perspectives. They inherited them. Their pronouncements on soccer have a genealogy that extends back to the 1880s in Australia.

There are very good reasons for the socio-political resentment of soccer. The game's reputation has legitimately suffered through fan violence and farcical organisational corruption around the world. Throughout world history it has been variously held responsible for the collapses of moral order and collective political will. It has been a game of the economic coloniser, imposing itself on or being taken up by indigenes who have thereby lost contact with their native customs. In Britain of ancient times, folk football, which is one significant forebear of all football codes, was even outlawed by monarchs afraid of the game's impact on their fighting forces.[17]

Each of these historical attitudes relates directly or indirectly to the main source of contemporary vilification – 'Soccerphobia', the fear of Association football and its supposed potential to damage national, regional and local cultures. The loudest bastions of soccerphobia are, curiously, found in Anglophone countries with a long and direct colonial connection to the British Isles – the birthplace of Association football. Australia, the United States of America, Canada, Ireland, New Zealand and South Africa all house strong and entrenched cultures of soccerphobia.

In three and a half of these countries, soccer is seen either as a threat to local and established games or as a game that cannot assimilate because of its foreignness or unsuitability. Ireland, Canada, the USA and southern and western Australia have developed regional variations of football (or other sports) that are assumed to be indigenous expressions of nationality – assumptions that are often flawed.

For example, baseball's claims to US indigenous status ignore the fact that it stems directly from games imported from Europe. The English game 'rounders' is a clear forerunner.[18] Often, claims of indigeneity rest more on politically expedient assertions of a given sport's purported relation to national independence and cultural difference than they do on historical fact. The antipathy to soccer rises and falls with waves of defensive nationalism.

In New Zealand, white South Africa and the Australian states of Queensland and New South Wales the local/imported divide is not as relevant – or at least it has less basis to be. The dominant football codes (Rugby Union or Rugby League) in each of these states or countries have clear British origins. Here, the disparagement of soccer tends to focus on questions of courage, masculinity and even sexuality. Historically, Association football has been seen as a game for degenerates, weaklings and 'poofters' across these sections of the soccerphobic world.

In recent times, the reality of sport-as-industry has been clarified. While organised elite sport for at least the past 100 years has had the element of profit-and-loss at its heart, for much of that history the ruling amateur mythology of sport provided a smokescreen, placing the economic realm into the category of a 'necessary evil'. Contemporary sports discourse happily brings questions of economics to bear. This newer general consciousness of sport as business is one that perceives any attempt to grow a sports market necessarily involves a diminution of another and competition among sports becomes a legitimate subject matter for sports discussion. Soccer's attempts to gain 'market share' in those regions like Australia, where historically it has been a subdominant sport, are one more economic basis for soccerphobia, a position that can dip into the toolbox of cultural soccerphobia as required.

To leave it at this would be to allow soccer to cry victim without accepting a deal of responsibility. Soccer often has only itself to blame. While the game has risen and fallen subject to external pressures, it has, in perhaps equal measure, been self-sabotaged by its internecine feuds and unfathomable incompetence across its history in Australia. For much of the period since 1958, the governing structure has encouraged horse trading and corrupt politics by allowing the tail to wag the dog as the game moved from club and state to national and international levels.

Historical factors are also crucial. Soccer has regularly collapsed under the massive weight of war and economic depression and often resurged on migrant tides. And while history has not been kind to the game in Australia, soccer has not made a good fist of becoming a narrative point of Australian history. Nor has it done a good job of remembering the times when was healthy and on the march.

## A NOTE ON USAGE

In recent years many proponents of soccer in Australia have begun to call the game football. In 2004 Football Federation Australia (FFA) replaced Soccer Australia as a part of sweeping reforms to the game's management and, in effect, 'took back' the name football – a move that received a deal of support in the soccer community but one that generated a great degree of opposition and disagreement from supporters of Australian Rules football and the Rugby codes.

This is understandable. 'Football' is a powerful term. Whenever it is used it also represents an incidental assertion of the hegemony of the game it is describing. 'Whoever owns that word,' wrote Martin Flanagan, 'to some extent owns the future.'[19]

Prior to 2004, in most of Victoria, Tasmania, South Australia and Western Australia 'football' denoted Australian Rules; in Queensland and New South Wales it usually meant Rugby League. And while generally these conventions still hold they have been destabilised by the re-naming of soccer. Significantly, the intense branding of terms like AFL (Australian Football League) and NRL (National Rugby League) has allowed soccer some space and leverage in adopting the term football. Some argue that Australian Rules needs to oppose soccer's attempt to call itself football because, in the words of Stephen Alomes, to 'surrender your name is to drop the ball – to weaken your standing, despite the dollar driven and marketing focus on "AFL".'[20]

Yet this new policy of soccer 'taking back' the name of football is based on a few fallacies:

- *The use of the term soccer was forced upon the game in Australia.* This is only partly true. In Australia the name soccer was adopted in order both to domesticate the game and to internationalise its image. The term British Association football was seen as tying the game too tightly to its British roots. The preferred option,

Association football, was unavailable, already taken by the Victorian Football Association (VFA), then the second-string Australia Rules competition in Victoria.[21] Soccer was the only term available that referenced Association football unambiguously.

- *Soccer is an American abomination.* This is not true. The term was invented in English public schools – though not necessarily without a pejorative aspect in that context.

- *Soccer is a diminutive that belittles the game.* This is a matter of emphasis and manner of articulation. Any diminution is in the manner of expression (soccer *is* a word that lends itself to sarcastic inflection) and not the semantic content.

- *Leading figures and commentators in the Australian game like Johnny Warren and Les Murray always used the word 'football' when talking about soccer.* They did not.

Confusion over names is part of the complex history of all football codes in Australia. Australian Rules and soccer have undergone significant name changes in the course of their development, as have their many organising and controlling bodies – usually for complicated cultural-political reasons.

As the rules of the Melbourne Football Club started their expansion out of Melbourne into other towns and colonies (including New Zealand) the name of the game became Melbourne Rules. This subsequently transformed into Victorian Rules and then Australian Rules (with a brief digression into Australasian Rules).[22] Today Australian Rules is officially known as Australian Football and also has made claims on the title of the 'National Game'.[23]

The game that was initially known in Victoria as Anglo-Australian football, or British Association rules, or English Association rules, and even Scottish Association rules, officially became soccer football in the 1920s and just plain soccer after that – though the *Argus* and other Victorian newspapers began to describe it as soccer from 1908 onwards. In Queensland the first organising body was the Anglo-Queensland

Football Association, while the game in New South Wales was initially administered by the English Football Association and then the Southern British Football Association, which was renamed the NSWFA in 1901 after Australian Rules relinquished that name. In the Perth press the game is described as 'soccer' for a few brief years around the turn of the century.

This represents a methodological problem for the historian – if the names of the games and their organising bodies are not consistent over time or across the various colonies at any given time, care needs to be taken when reading an historical newspaper article that refers to football.

For example, articles in a Maitland newspaper in 1883 refer to matches of Association football played by a team named Northumberland.[24] A reader today could be forgiven for the immediate assumption that it was a soccer team composed of miners from the north east of England. Closer reading shows that it was actually a game of Victorian Rules being played by a local Maitland team against South Melbourne FC. In 1894 a game 'was played on the Albion Ground, West Maitland, under Association rules, between the Northumberland and Redfern (Sydney) teams. The match was won by the former by 2 points to nil'.[25] This match also seems to have been played under Victorian Rules even though the name 'Association rules' would have signified soccer in most other parts of Australia.

This changeability of names points to a very different conception of football from the ones held today – the idea that soccer and rugby and Australian Rules were differing strains of the same 'British game of football'. For much of the first part of the twentieth century, newspaper soccer reports were made under the heading of football. Typically, the Melbourne *Argus* would list under the heading of football: VFL, VFA, soccer and rugby. And while they gave greater weight to Australian Rules there was not the same sense of separation that the media deploys today.

In some newspapers, the football results were given in such an order that the game being played can only be discerned from the recorded scores. This too represents a methodological problem. Soccer reports are often there in newspapers, but they are sometimes buried at the end of or hidden within a general football report. Historians may have overlooked vital pieces of information because of this.

From 1850 until about 1870 many reports of football games across Australia were published in which virtually all that is documented is that between zero and three goals were scored, mostly kicked but occasionally taken across the line in or by a scrimmage. Journalists thought little of posterity when they filed their reports. Different kinds of football were being played, but usually there is no indication of what kind.

The FFA's rebranding of soccer as 'football' threatens to introduce the same kind of lack of clarity for historians of the future. Therefore I am an advocate for the use of soccer in public discourse for the time being – at least until history and common sense determines otherwise.

In this book I will tend to use the term soccer – unless context requires the use of Association football. Where possible I will allow reports from the time to name the game as they will – in any combination of (British, English, London or Scottish) Association (rules, football, game).

If this seems unwieldy, a further complication is introduced by the broad use of the terms Association and League by Australian Rules in Melbourne and elsewhere, especially in relation to the Victorian Rules-playing NSW Football Association. Another source of confusion is the seemingly obstinate refusal of media from the Australian Rules states to get the names of the other codes right, periodically confusing the two codes of rugby with each other and either with soccer, thereby creating minor headaches for the football historian.

In relation to the non-soccer codes of football I will use the following practice:

- Australian Rules will be referred to as Melbourne Rules, Victorian Rules or Australian Rules depending on the historical period.

- Rugby Union and Rugby League will be used post-split. Before that I will refer to Rugby. Sometimes it will also be appropriate to use the term 'rugby codes' when referring to both games simultaneously.

- Rugby League is the least problematical, apart from when it is called, briefly, Northern Union.

# CHAPTER 1

# WAITING FOR ASSOCIATION FOOTBALL

The great historian of the counter-narrative, EP Thompson, famously claimed the English working class 'did not rise like the sun at an appointed time. It was present at its own making'.[26] It might be argued that soccer did not arrive in Australia at an appointed time. It was present at its own arrival. Even as soccer was 'getting off the boat' in its organised Brisbane, Hobart and Sydney manifestations, soccer was already here in the shadowy presence of its pre-figurative forms and isolated kickers.

Football had been played by settlers and soldiers in the 1820s, and footballs had been imported and sold commercially from the 1830s.[27] Generally we have little explicit idea of how these games were played. Variations of kicking, handling, non-handling and running football games, codes derived from English public schools and local games across Britain and Ireland, many of which are now forgotten, were played across Australia well into the 1870s. Many of these included small-sided predominantly kicking games played for money or other tangible rewards. These games were sometimes more like soccer as codified in 1863 than the 'mayhem in the villages' of England with which they are often confused or amalgamated.[28]

Even in Victoria, where an early version of Victorian Rules was codified in 1866, football as practised was a repository of rule confusion until the formation of the Victorian Football Association (VFA) in 1877 and even afterwards.[29] Nonetheless, a conventional narrative has come to dominate the popular story of Australian football, and despite the chaos and fluidity of those early forms of football, soccer is assumed to be spiritually absent in Australian life until 1880. The reasons for the development of such a narrative are varied and complex. It is only with the recent on-line digitisation of searchable Australian newspaper archives that ample countervailing evidence has been effectively available.

For example, a report in the *Brisbane Courier* on a football game in Brisbane in 1866 bemoaned the level of ball- and man-handling and argued that the game would be better if the players focused on kicking the ball:

> About thirty members of the Brisbane Football Club mustered in the Queen's Park in the afternoon, and a game was got up. Though the majority of players were out of practice or unaccustomed to kicking the football, several very exciting contests ensued, and the goals were not kicked without a hard struggle. The rules were not very strictly adhered to, and many of the players used their hands more than their feet.[30]

Similarly, a report in the *Queenslander* on a game held in 1868 implies that the convention is *against* handling the ball except when preparatory to a kick:

> There were several severe 'scrimmages' in the course of the afternoon, and two or three of the players were slightly hurt, but not sufficiently to necessitate their retirement from the field. If the rules of the club, with respect to holding players and handling the ball, were more closely adhered to, better and less dangerous games would be the result.[31]

In 1869 an absurd match between Sydney University and the crew of the vessel *Rosario* saw the former side follow the Rugby rules while the latter appeared to be playing some other game. After one journalist recommended that subsequent games be played under the rules 'put forward by the London Association', the teams met again a week later.[32] The ball was thrice kicked between the posts, but goals were not awarded because the ball travelled *over* the crossbar each time.[33] Can it be assumed that this game was therefore played under new rules, perhaps similar to the ones advocated?

A year later a match report of a game in Sydney was published that included the sentence: 'For the Engineers Lieut S. Fuller displayed some very good dribbling, and we were glad to see "the Major" had not lost his charging propensities; the goal-keeping of Capt Merriman was also first-rate.'[34]

Are these games of soccer? It cannot be said for certain. But nor can it be said that they are not, especially as they present descriptions and language that would be perfectly in keeping with a game of Association football at the time.

And what relation does the following game, recollected in a letter to the editor of the Adelaide *Register* by 'One of the Old School' 53 years after its occurrence, have to the game of Association football?:

> As an intimate and almost lifelong acquaintance of the late Mr. John Acraman, I was pleased to peruse the interesting account of his career published in *The Register* last week. Among the various points which attracted my attention particularly was that in regard to Mr Acraman's association with athletics and sports, especially football. It is quite true that he was the first man to introduce football properly into South Australia, and that he had five round balls sent out from England. He also erected the first set of goalposts. That was over 50 years ago – to be exact, in 1854. As there were no rival clubs the pioneer 'hunters of the leather,' who included numerous St. Peter's College old boys, picked sides. The combats took place on the park lands between the Frome Road and City under what were known as the Harrow rules. The goalposts were about 9 ft high with a bar across the top. The ball had to be kicked below this, and could not be handled except when being marked. Shouldering was permitted, but holding and hacking were strictly prohibited. The teams usually comprised 20 men each.[35]

This game appears to be very close to Association rules as they came to be drawn up in the 1860s. The main point of difference is not the mark but the crossbar, which was not introduced into soccer until 1875. If this match occurred as the letter-writer remembered, it could mean that soccer in South Australia was established early on, only to be later supplanted by a form of Victorian cultural imperialism.[36]

One of the difficulties of writing football histories is that there are few, if any, accurate visual images of games as they were played in the nineteenth century. When it comes to the Adelaide Harrow game a kind of visual time capsule is available because as a public-school game it has probably changed little in 150 years. Football historian Stephen Bailey writes that while 'details of the rules have changed from those of the 1840s ... the characteristics of Harrow Football, the Eton Field Game, and Winchester Football remain largely the same as the games played at the beginning of Queen Victoria's reign.' He believes that 'an investigation of the football codes played at these three schools will reveal a line of continuity and similarity which has not been acknowledged so far.'[37] Contemporary video recordings of Harrow football are available and if Bailey's argument can be taken at face value then they represent a window into how that game was played in the 1850s. It is not a long stretch to see Harrow football as a progenitor of soccer.[38]

'One of the Old School' goes on to trace the transformation of Adelaide football, seeing a smooth transition from the Harrow game through the Kensington Rules into Victorian Rules. Regrettably, he fails to acknowledge the brief adoption of English Association rules at a meeting of delegates from three Adelaide clubs in 1873, at which 'a code was drawn up somewhat similar to the rules of the English Football Association.'[39]

The rules were advocated and adopted in Adelaide in 1873 and competitive games were attempted in 1873 and 1874. Turmoil ensued when a number of players refused to adhere to the non-handling prohibition, thereby rendering the games farcical. 'Several interesting football matches have been held during the month,' reported the Melbourne *Argus*. 'The alterations in the rules have been found to work satisfactorily, but the rule against handling the ball is still too much disregarded.'[40]

This lacuna shows that the memories are indeed ones 'of the old school' and are necessarily vague, but it nonetheless intimates a radically alternative history of football in Adelaide and throughout Australia. It also bears considering that the early development narratives of other codes have been built on equally flimsy practical evidence of games that bear much less similarity to the eventually established code than this example does to soccer.

By 1876 something resembling Victorian Rules had come to be established in Adelaide, with a ball that was 'oval instead of round' and without 'the crossbar and rope at the goals'.[41] And even though the round ball made a comeback just a month later[42], the dismantling of the crossbar ensured the move to Victorian Rules had been inaugurated. Still, in 1878 one letter writer to the *South Australian Advertiser* argued that soccer was 'football proper' and 'not nearly so dangerous' as other codes.[43]

## SOCCER ADVOCACY

The descriptions of football games in Australia are vague and their lack of focus on the mechanics and rules of play is frustrating. On the other hand a counterpoint clarity of argument is demonstrated by the advocates of English, British, London or Scottish Association rules in various newspaper pieces. Their entreaties seem to begin around 1867, four years after the formation of the Football Association (FA) in England. They lead to the aforementioned Adelaide example and games of soccer in Woogaroo, Brisbane in 1875 and Hobart in 1879 before rising to a high pitch in Sydney in 1880, producing the first organised and sustained competition in Australia.[44]

Versions of Association rules were advocated on occasion by correspondents to newspaper editors around the colonies, urging the football authorities to adopt a form of the game for a wide variety of reasons. It was considered to have a number of advantages, being: safer, more sensible, more comprehensible, less chaotic, better, more 'scientific' or more orderly than other versions of football being played all around Australia at that time.

'I must here say that the code of rules under which these matches are played, a strange combination of Rugby and other rules, is not by any means the best that could be selected,' wrote one correspondent to *Bell's Life in Sydney and Sporting Chronicle* in 1867. He felt that it 'would be far better ... to discard at once these now generally condemned laws, and play under those of the English Football Association or the joint Oxford and Cambridge Rules, both of which are decidedly superior and much more comprehensible.'[45]

A few weeks later the same writer reiterated his argument:

Prior to next season a revision of the rules would be in my opinion very expedient, and much of the Rugby ball *handling*, which renders the game not *football*, and mainly contributes to these useless mauls, might with very great advantage be then got rid of.[46]

On 21 August 1869 the following piece appeared in *Bell's Life in Sydney and Sporting Chronicle* arguing for the immediate application on the 'London Association' rules:

For the use of [the Rugby] Code in its entirety, I am no advocate, as in my opinion it sanctions handling the ball in a manner hardly suggestive of FOOTBALL; still even the Rugby rules are more definite than those under which Saturday's match was contested. In all future matches, however I trust that the University will adopt the short set of rules – given in MCMAHON'S CRICKET AND SPORTS MANUAL – as they are taken from those put forward by the London Association, and those now used by the two Universities of Oxford and Cambridge. They are specially simple, and are, at the same time, explicit and comprehensive.[47]

While not explicitly arguing for Association rules, a writer in *Australian Town and Country Journal* in May 1870 suggested the adoption of the FA rule whereby 'handling the ball under any pretence what ever shall be prohibited'[48], a change that would effectively turn any game of football into soccer, in everything but name.

In Queensland, the Petrie-terrace club in Brisbane adopted Association rules in 1876. The *Brisbane Courier* complained:

The Brisbane and Rangers Football Clubs have adopted the Rugby Union rules, while the New Petrie-terrace Club intend to go by the London Association rules. Now in matches between the clubs, each one practising under his own rules, this will cause great confusion. Would it not be better for the clubs to meet and fix on some rules to be followed by all Brisbane clubs? All the clubs in Sydney have adopted the Rugby Union.[49]

The Petrie club soon relinquished the Association rules and took up Rugby in line with the other clubs.[50] This is probably explained by the fact that at this time Rugby is at the apogee of its popularity in England, much more popular than soccer by some criteria. Migrants coming to New South Wales and Queensland in these years might well have had more knowledge of Rugby.

Still, there were those in Brisbane who wanted a non-handling game. A month later a correspondent to the *Brisbane Courier* recalled his 'Harrow play in '38–39':

> the ball was never touched by the hand from the time it
> was thrown up and kicked off by the captain of the side
> winning the toss until it had passed the goal or base.
> Hands were thrown out to save the risk of broken bones,
> or, rather, the forearm as far as the chin, but otherwise were
> kept close to the side, as in running matches, and the play
> kept entirely to the feet.[51]

Even in Victoria, a few infrequent correspondents seemed passionate in their advocacy of Association rules. In 1869 a self-confessed Rugby man, 'Old Harrovian', argued that he was 'satisfied that the best game for a club is that of the Football Association'. He claimed that is 'the easiest learnt, the least rough, and contains certain elements of other existing games which make it the best adapted to a mixed body of players'.[52]

In 1873 'Trojan' wrote to the *Argus* 'to throw out a few suggestions for the consideration of club committees':

> The game, as played here, may perhaps exhibit strength and
> courage on the part of the players but (to my mind) very
> little of science, law, or order and is productive of many
> and serious accidents as the events of the past season testify;
> and were these the only objections I am of [the] opinion
> that could a reform be introduced which should not in any
> degree lessen the exciting interest of the game but add to
> the safety of the players, it is deserving of the favourable
> consideration of those holding a prominent position
> among the practical lovers of the sport. Let our local clubs
> but witness a contest of the Wasps versus Zingari or other

celebrated London clubs and they would see a game played
which while as full of interest to players and spectators and
calling for far more actual scientific judgment and skill, is
not liable to one tenth the danger of our style. As played at
home (or in London) the game is essentially football, not
indiscriminate scrimmage. The London Football Association
rules provide a certain distance between goals, between the
posts of each goal, the height of goal posts, and that a tape
be stretched across the posts of a goal under which and
between the posts the ball must be kicked by the foot before
a goal is won; that before kicking off the players take their
respective sides off the ball, and do not mix themselves up;
that the goals be defended by their respective sides without
unfair hindrance from their antagonists (in Melbourne I
notice a player of the opposite side may stand at his enemy's
goal to receive the ball, and kick it in); that neither the ball
nor the players be handled (some clubs modify this rule by
allowing a free kick for fair catch and mark only). Charging
is of course permitted but without the use of the hands, and
no tripping, hacking, &c.

Do you not think Sir, that the officers of the various local
clubs should meet and consider the advisability of some
such regulations for the game here, so that the next season
may possess all the interest without fear of the disasters of
the past?[53]

A year later another letter appeared (written by C.C.[54]), this time with
the laws of the FA appended:

I am glad to see your leader of this morning on the game
of football. As an onlooker, I have seen the objectionable
features you refer to, and my opinion is that they are
altogether attributable to the practice of the players picking
up the ball and attempting to run with it. If a strict rule
were made against touching the ball with the hand, except
to catch, when a free kick should be allowed as at present,
we should not hear much of brutality in connection with
this necessarily rather rough game.[55]

Another letter, written by 'S.G.H.' appeared in the *Argus* five years later in 1879 under the heading 'English and Australian Football'. Given that organised soccer in Melbourne was only four years away, this may be a recommendation from an eventual participant in the game:

> Having witnessed the game played to-day [9 August] between the Melbourne and Geelong Clubs, kindly allow me to make a suggestion which I have no doubt, if carried into effect, will be an improvement on the Victorian game. My suggestion is that the association rules, as played in the old country with the greatest success, should at least be tried here, so that the public can judge for themselves between the two. Being myself a member of the Queen's-park Football Club, Glasgow, I should like to see the association rules introduced into the colony, and for myself have no doubt of their ultimately being a success. The association rules mean simply football alone – that is, there is no handling the ball at all, except by the goalkeepers, and a player touching the ball with his hand, the opposite side claim a free kick. It is a pleasanter game to witness than the Victorian game, as brute force which, I think, and here no doubt many others will endorse what I say, predominates too much in the Victorian game, is to a certain extent dispensed with where the association rules are played. My proposal is that the Melbourne clubs in the spirit of fair play should take the matter up and play a few games, and I shall be most happy to provide them with the rules, if not already in their possession. Of course the association game will be a new feature in the colony, and as the Victorian game has obtained a great hold on the public, I should like that all prejudice should be put aside so as to allow the new game to be thoroughly tried. I may mention that the association rules have taken precedence over the Rugby rules in Scotland and are gradually becoming the favourite game in England.[56]

It received an immediate response from 'A. Clergyman':

Your correspondent 'SGH' is of [the] opinion that football according to the Association rules is a better game than that which has developed under our Victorian sky. He suggests that the former should be tried here. It is a very fair suggestion. The Rugby game has, I believe, been witnessed in Melbourne. Let the Association rules be tried as well, that our rising players may have an opportunity of judging for themselves. But I risk the opinion, as an old Melbourne footballer, after seeing some good matches played at Blackheath, that the Victorian game is preferable to either of the English ones. The Rugby game consists almost entirely of handling – the Association permits no handling, or hardly any – while football in Melbourne has happily developed along the *via media*, combining plenty of handling with plenty of kicking. I think if our players were appealed to they would pronounce both games to be less 'scientific' than our own, and quite as dangerous.[57]

This is an expression of the idea of Victorian Rules as the middle-road, and perhaps a hybrid and derivative, code. The correspondent asserts Melbourne Rules' scientific superiority, and if not a game of the soil, then one developed under the Victorian sky. Association rules had its advocates but it also had its antagonists. Significantly, soccer is declared *in absentia* just as dangerous as local football.

Despite the frequent urging in Sydney it is not until 1878 that a report is published there on a practical application of FA rules, in a half-and-half soccer/rugby game played in Sydney:

A football match, between Old Victorian Players and All-comers, was played on Saturday at Moore Park. It was intended to show the relative merits of football as played by the English Association rules and the game as played under Rugby rules. About 3000 spectators witnessed the sport. The play resulted in a draw, with a slight advantage on the side of the All-comers.[58]

The half-and-half game suggests that clubs and players in some parts of Australia were able to be flexible and keep something of an open mind on football codes and laws. Moreover, it makes it clear that the games had not yet ossified into their camps.

But it also demonstrates that football authorities were not yet convinced of the viability of English Association rules; it was not until the 1880s that sustained and regularised soccer associations began.

## WAITING FOR SOCCER

Given the level of advocacy and interest as expressed by correspondents to the newspapers, why does it take so long for Association football to be played on an organised and regular basis in Australia? One explanation might be that this was a period of relatively low inward migration, after the Victorian Gold Rush and before the Western Australian boom and the full impact of the Great Depression in the United Kingdom. It is not until the 1880s that migration picks up and a critical mass of people with a soccer consciousness arrives to satisfy the competitive desire of the soccer advocates. That being said, the patterns of migration differed from colony to colony. The strong waves of migration into New South Wales between 1860 and 1890 in all likelihood carried with them more individuals and groups with the desire to play rugby or soccer. In contrast Victoria (and its nascent football code) remained relatively protected from British migration and its two main football codes.[59]

Or should the question be about why it takes the game so long to be reported on in newspapers? Did the advocates and their kind retreat into their shells or did they conduct informal 'round-ball' non-handling pick-up games on open ground across Australia? While they might well have conducted informal games, this was not something to which press attention would be drawn. This remains speculation until evidence is available. Roy Hay, perhaps Australia's foremost soccer historian, believes that it was 'ignorance rather than malevolence that initially resulted in the absence of references to pre-existing football in Victoria.' Whichever forms of football were in existence prior to and alongside Melbourne/Victorian rules they were effectively 'eliminated from public consciousness' by ignorant, myopic and partisan journalists.[60]

The problem is one of discussing the practice of something for which no published direct textual evidence exists. However, the necessary equipment, players and mutually understood rules for the successful prosecutions of games of Association football were indeed in place.

## EQUIPMENT

As long as men had coats they had goal posts.[61] Grounds to play on were also readily available, even though their quality was questionable. The infernal ground wars of the twentieth century were a long way off. Balls were a different matter. Soccer cannot be played without a more or less spherical ball that bounces more or less truly. Were these available in Australia? 'Foot Balls' were available for sale in Sydney as early as 1837 and 1838[62], but their specifications are unclear.

There was no shortage of round balls in Australia between 1860 and 1880. They were imported and available for retail sale around the country, as the following advertisements from the 1860s indicate. A clear distinction is made, indicating that both oval and round balls could be purchased. In Sydney in 1866 McMahons sold 'footballs, rugby and other shapes'.[63] In Launceston in 1865: 'MESSRS. J. WALCH & SONS . . . received a supply of foot-balls, including the new "Rugby" shape'.[64] And in Melbourne in 1862, George Marshall and Co, cricketing depot, Swanston-street advertised: 'FOOTBALLS, ex Kent – A large assortment of Rugby and other FOOTBALLS'.[65] Indeed, in 1863 and 1864 it appears quite difficult to obtain non-round balls in Melbourne: the 'only Rugby BALLS at present in Melbourne are at E. Quiney's, 1071 Swanston street', if the advertisement is to be believed.[66]

In Hobart in 1873 J. Walch and Sons placed the following advertisement in the Hobart *Mercury*[67]:

BEST LONDON MADE FOOTBALLS.
Stout Leather with India Rubber Bags.
No. 1. Round. Full match size.          20/.
No. 2. Round. Medium size.          17/6.
No. 3. Round. Small Size.          15/.
No. 4. Rugby shape. Full match size.          20/.

Six years later, in 1879, the same balls are available but the order is inverted, perhaps indicating the rising influence of the Victorian Rules[68]:

New Supplies of the Best Quality London and Rugby
Footballs, Just Received.
No. 1. Rugby-Oval-Full Match Size.          21/0

No. 2. Rugby-Oval-Second Size.            17/0
No. 3. London-Round-Full Match Size.  20/0
No. 4. London-Round-Second Size.        17/6
No. 5. London-Round-Third Size.          15/0

We might infer a shortage of balls of any kind in Launceston in 1860 if the following classified advertisement is any guide:

> STOLEN from the racecourse, during the Boys' Parade,
> a large football, covered with leather, and quite new,
> belonging to the Boys' Corps. It was taken by a man in a
> check jumper, with brown wideawake hat. Five shillings
> reward will be paid for the discovery of the thief.[69]

Even in Melbourne, where soccer was not played formally until 1883, round balls were still available in 1879, a good while after Victorian Rules had universally adopted the rugby ball in the late 1860s. In 1879 the *Footballer*[70] advertised:

> FOOTBALLS:
> Gilbert's Best Rugby – 15s each by taking the half dozen
> Insides and Covers Sold Separate in all sizes
> Boy's Round and Rugby-shape
> 5s 6d to 10s 6d.

To what use would these round balls be put by the boys (and adults) who played with them?

## PLAYERS

Not only were round balls available, a sizeable proportion of the general football-playing population preferred them. This preference is not merely a matter of taste. It is a preference with practical implications. A round ball tends to lead to a ground-based, dribbling or kicking game rather than an aerial or running game. This may go some way to explaining the following controversy from 1865:

> The Carlton Club ascribe their defeat to the fact that they
> were obliged to play with the oval, or Rugby ball, while
> they had always been accustomed to a round ball; and they
> complain that their opponents would not allow a round ball
> to be introduced even after they had won the first goal.[71]

In 1865 not only did the Carlton players prefer the round ball they were perhaps unfamiliar and certainly less competent with the rugby ball in use elsewhere at the time. As *The National Game*, perhaps the most comprehensive history of Australian Rules, explains, 'the issue of the shape of the ball was not really settled for many years to come, for the next two decades [from 1860] there were reports of spherical rather than oval balls in use'.[72]

In August 1876 Adelaide footballers expressed a strong preference for the round ball, even after having adopted the oval one a month earlier. At a 'meeting of delegates from football clubs to arrange a code of playing rules [it] was determined unanimously to play with the round ball in preference to the oval one'.[73]

## RULES

The rules of the FA were available within Australia shortly after they were formulated and subsequently in their newly modified iterations. They were brought into Australia and were published occasionally as rule books, and in annuals, magazines and newspapers and were broadly known within the football-playing community. Moreover, many old players brought with them their own remembrances of Association, Harrow, Eton, Cambridge and regional rules.

J. Walch and Sons in Hobart sold more than balls. They also sold books of football rules. At the foot of the 1879 advertisement for balls referred to above they advertised a 'just published' English football publication: 'FOOTBALL and HOW TO PLAY IT'. [74] Code unclear, the only reasonable certainty is that the book did not contain the Victorian Rules. In all probability it documented at least both FA and Rugby rules.

The 1878 edition of the *Footballer* contained a brief but reasonable history of Association football from its formation in 1863 until the time of writing. It also presented the FA rules for Melbourne readers. Why?

Was this history simply filler for a publication short of content or was it a response to a demand for Association rules in Melbourne?

## A VISION OF SOCCER

Can a legitimate vision of people playing (incipient[75]) soccer in the period 1860–1880 be constructed from this circumstantial evidence?

Perhaps the contemporary practices of Melbourne's *Age* and *Herald Sun* newspapers add another dimension to the argument. They certainly raise the question of how seriously to take newspapers as indicators of the extent and strength of a particular social practice.

The newspapers contain little to no record of soccer played in Melbourne in winter 2017, organised or informal. They effectively obliterate the more than 60,000 people playing organised soccer and Futsal in contemporary Victoria. Their soccer coverage is limited to so-called 'top-tier' versions of the sport: the Australian national team and the (summer-based) A-League, the English Premier League, the European Champions League and international competitions like the European National Championship and World Cups. And yet other forms of evidence and experience make it clear that organised and informal games of soccer flourish around the city. As newspapers of record, their refusal to perform what some might see as their public duty is a nonetheless useful reminder that an absence of reports does not mean the absence of a game, flourishing or otherwise.

The idea of Joe Honeysett and his sons practising with a soccer ball on the 'village green'[76] in New Norfolk, north of Hobart, in 1906, enjoining his neighbours to come and play until they have enough players to challenge the crew of a visiting vessel is one that prompts the imagining of earlier, Victorian correlatives. Honeysett's story, noted by historians such as David Young, Chris Hudson and others, is known because he is a relatively prominent figure in Tasmanian and Australian soccer history. The nameless, recordless soccer players of Victoria remain unknown.[77]

## SOCCER IN VICTORIA

Of the Australian colonies in the period 1860–1880 Victoria was the one in which English Association rules seemed the least present – whether as a discussion point or as embodied practice. The occasional advocacies aside, soccer is historiographically absent.[78] Yet the following Melbourne report of a game played in 1870 seems to discuss a contest that looks a lot like soccer:

> An amusing game of football will be played on the Metropolitan ground, Yarra-park, this afternoon, between the local club and a team chosen from the ranks of the Victorian police force, who will play under the guidance of Mr J Conway, of the Carlton Club. The game will be played something after the home style, and holding or running with the ball will not be allowed.[79]

When the police team and Melbourne FC were scheduled to have a match it was felt that major rule modifications were needed to give the police team a chance to be competitive. As a result the game was to be played according to the 'home rules'.[80] The report followed two days later. The Melbourne team had proved too strong for the Police, who struggled to cope despite the modifications. The match, which was described as 'a most amusing affair', attracted a large crowd:

> The toss was won by the police, who elected to kick down the hill. With the view of equalising the chances of the teams, the rules of the Melbourne Club were slightly departed from, neither 'marks,' holding, nor running with the ball being allowed.[81]

It is difficult to work out just what this game might have looked like. The Melbourne Rules of the time need to be imagined with three crucial departures. Players could possibly handle the ball, but they could not claim a mark, hold on to it or run with it. Most likely they needed to kick it quickly after catching it to avoid being pummelled.

The notions of 'home style' and 'home rules' are intriguing. The various prohibitions and the absence of offside rule out Rugby and many of the public-school games. The absence of offside would also rule out Association football as codified in 1863, although it would not rule out a soccer-like game. If anything the 'home' game they most closely resemble is the football of the Sheffield Rules, a game that is formative in the development of soccer, though it, too, allowed a mark.

Ultimately, it cannot yet be said one way or the other if this is an early example of a soccer-derived game being played in Australia. Despite its being a close relative, neither can this modified game be claimed as an immediate progenitor of Australian soccer.[82]

Whereas AFL and Rugby historians are sometimes quick to colonise early generic references to football, soccer historians lack an established narrative mythology and the confidence this might provide in claiming the Melbourne–police game for soccer history. As it stands, this particular game and many others from around Australia lie under erasure, unbelonging in generic football history. Too difficult to categorise. And still too easy to ignore.

# CHAPTER 2

# THE 'CHIMERA' OF ORIGINS

In July 1880 a movement in Sydney seemed to crystallise. A number of letters to the editor of the *Sydney Morning Herald* were published, advocating the playing of football under the English Association rules.[83]

This long letter from John Walter Fletcher published in the *Sydney Morning Herald* on July 17, 1880 summed up the level of interest and took the important step of suggesting a meeting:

> Sir, - I was glad to see in your issue of this morning a letter advocating the introduction of the English Association game into New South Wales, and I am a little surprised that some old English player has not made the suggestion before. I have reason to think from conversations I have had on the subject that if the game could properly be started it would become very popular, not only with players, but with the public. Unfortunately, a very general misapprehension appears to exist as to the nature of the game, a great many people I have spoken to evidently confusing it with the Victorian Association game[84], whereas the two games have not a single point in common. As to its chances of popularity, let any one read in *Bell's Life* the accounts of International or club contests in Glasgow, Sheffield, London, &c. witnessed often by from 10,000 to 12,000 spectators. It is, I think, about twelve years since the game was first started in England, though its principle, that football is a game for feet and for hands,

had long existed in the Eton and Harrow games. At the present time the football players of Great Britain, playing under Rugby and Association rules, are about equally divided, and the two games exist side by side without one interfering in the least with the other, save that of late the value of good dribbling has become universally acknowledged in the Rugby game. I feel that we are rather late in writing in advocacy of the English Association game, inasmuch as a large section of the football players of New South Wales, dissatisfied with Rugby rules, appear to have committed themselves to the adoption of Victorian Rules. Nevertheless, there must be many old English and Scotch Association players, or old Eton and Harrow men, who would be glad to see their old game played here, and who would make an effort to introduce it; and I am quite sure that the principle of the game, which forbids the use of the hands, except by goalkeeper, and does away with scrummaging, collaring, mauling, &c, will commend itself to a very large section or this community. The game is essentially a scientific one, requiring, above everything else, unselfish and organized combination. I do not wish to attack the old Rugby game, which, properly played, is interesting and exciting to players and spectators; but must enter a protest against the introduction of the Victorian game, which, though certainly interesting and amusing to look at, is, I believe, rougher than the Rugby, and violates the fundamental principle of all games like football – I mean the law of off side. The very thing condemned under the name of 'sneaking' in the Eton game is here encouraged and applauded, and in fact may almost be said to be the chief art of the game. In the brief space of a letter it is impossible to say all that one would in behalf of the introduction of the rules of the English Association; but I hope that, since at the present time a radical change is demanded in the present code, football players and the public generally will give the matter a more thorough investigation than it has yet received before committing

themselves to the Victorian game. I should be willing to
communicate with gentlemen willing to assist in starting
a club under the rules of the English Association, and
perhaps it might be possible to convene a meeting to
consider the whole question. I am, &c.,
J. W. FLETCHER.
Union Club, July 14.[85]

This is a remarkable and important letter, one that has claims to be a
kind of founding document along the lines of Tom Wills' letter to the
editor of *Bell's Sporting Life in Victoria* in 1858 in which he advocated the
formation of a football club (or, failing that, a rifle club) in Melbourne.
Wills' letter is generally understood to be the wellspring of Australian
Rules football.[86]

Fletcher believed a large participation and spectator base existed for
Association football in New South Wales that was as yet untapped and
unsatisfied. The potential contributors to the game came from the English
and 'Scotch' Associations or Eton and Harrow. He also made it clear that
the Victorian Rules, which would later develop into Australian Rules, was
an oppositional code with 'not a single point' in common with Association
football.[87] The letter picked no fight with Rugby, seeing the possibility of
the two codes subsisting. Directly, a meeting was convened for 3 August
by Fletcher and J A Todd. Its purpose was 'to consider and promote the
introduction of football under English Association rules'. Therefore, all
'football players and others who may be interested in the improvement of
the winter pastime are invited to attend'.[88]

The plan was not to supplant Rugby but to benefit football generally by,
firstly, introducing Association rules and, secondly, staving off the challenge
from Victorian Rules. Two weeks later, the first game was played and the
*Sydney Morning Herald* reported:

> The first match in New South Wales played under English
> Association rules was played on Saturday last, by the newly
> formed club, against the King's School boys at Parramatta.
> The visitors had a very fair team, allowing for the fact that
> hardly one of them had played football for some years.
> This advantage was, however, balanced by the fact that

the boys had not played these rules before. The game was well contested for an hour and a half, and terminated in favour of the visitors by five goals to none; the number of goals must not, however, be taken as a criterion of the play, which was remarkably even, particularly after half time, the boys on several occasions only failing to score on account of their want of familiarity with the art of passing and middling the ball. On the side of the English Association Club all played up well, but the play of D. Roxburgh as back was remarkably good and invaluable to his side, and Scott's goal-keeping deserves praise. On the King's School side the play of Fenwick was very fine, and he would make a grand Association player; all, however, played well. Mr Savage, an old International player, played with and coached King's School. The names of the club players were – J.A Todd (captain), W.J. Baker, J.W. Fletcher, C.E. Hewlett, C.F. Fletcher, Wastinage, W. Robertson, W. Simson, Chapman, D. Roxburgh, J. Scott (goal).

The article concluded by pointing out that a further 'match has been arranged, under English Association rules, on Moore Park, for next Saturday, against the Redfern Club'.[89]

The new team did not yet have a name, a situation that was rectified at a 'committee meeting of the newly-formed English Association Football Club' on August 19 at which 'The Wanderers' were christened. A number of decisions were ratified at the meeting, along with the crucial ambition to obtain membership of the English Football Association. They were:

1  'That the club be called "The Wanderers." '

2  'That the uniform be white jersey and cap, with badge southern cross, and blue stockings.'

3  'That an account of the proceedings be sent to England to the secretary of the English Association, for publication.'

4  'That the club be enrolled (with permission) in the English Association'.[90]

The first game under the new name saw the team score another win, this time against a team from the Rugby club, Redfern FC:

> The second match under the English Association Rules took place at Moore Park on Saturday last, and resulted in a win for the newly-named Wanderers by two goals to nil, both of which were secured in the first 10 minutes, after which the game was very even. Redfern Club, being strangers to the rules, played up well, ably assisted by W.J. Baker. For Redfern, J. Mulcahy and North played well, whilst for the Wanderers J. Fletcher, Harbottle, and M'Donald, were in grand form.[91]

About this well-coordinated series of events a conventional and robust narrative has emerged: a club with a name, colours and rules to play by; a series of games played and planned; a desire to affiliate with the FA in England; and something resembling the founding document/moment so beloved of many football historians are all in place. Australian soccer had kicked off.

But the story is wrong. The narrative details may be correct, but the idea of a starting point is wide of the mark. Unfortunately for the 'Sydney-origin' thesis, a similar series of events had occurred in the colony of Tasmania's main city, Hobart, one year before, albeit on a smaller scale.

## HOBART, 1879

The Hobart *Mercury* of 28 April 1879 reported on the City Football Club's AGM and its adoption of the 'rules of the British Football Association':

> The annual general meeting of members of the City Football Club was held on Saturday evening at the Town Hall. Mr. J.R. Betts took the chair. The attendance was good at first, but the proceedings being of a protracted nature, the members dwindled very much towards the finish. The committee recommended the adoption of a fresh code of playing rules, as the present code entirely

prevented the club from meeting any foreign team. The rules of the British Football Association, with the addition of the drop kick, were recommended. The following officers were elected: – Captain, Captain Boddam; vice-captains, Messrs, Molloy and Pitfield; secretary, Mr. A.D. Watchorn; treasurer, Mr. Lindley; committee, Messrs. Lovett, Finlay, and Paul.[92]

Captain Edmond Meyer Tudor-Boddam is a central figure in this decision. Boddam had arrived in Hobart via Sydney in May 1878 to take up a post as 'Brigade-Major to the corps', the main function of which was to control public-works projects.[93] An Anglo-Indian and noted cricketer and footballer, he insisted that an English code of football be adopted for the winter months. He had played rugby in Sydney and seemed concerned to adopt a football code that would enable a sporting commerce with England (and New South Wales) rather than Victoria.

It is clear that many City members were unhappy with this decision and Captain Boddam soon found himself on the outer. Undaunted, Boddam moved over to the Cricketers FC of Hobart where he directly influenced its decision to adopt the Association code. The Cricketers voted 10–9 to adopt English Association Rules at their meeting on 5 May.[94] Boddam and his seconder would have preferred Rugby but acknowledged that its rules were too complex. Both were derisory about Victorian Rules.[95]

Under his guidance, the Cricketers began their season with an internal scratch match, played under English Association Rules, on 10 May 1879. The sides were picked by F V Smith and G S Chapman:

> Chapman's side proved victorious by two goals to one, both kicked by B. Stuart, well judged kicks. H.B. Smith with a good piece of dribbling secured the goal for the other side. Besides the goal kickers, the most prominent players were Boddam, F.V. Smith, Chapman, R. Kirby, H. Prior, L. M'Leod and Davenport (the last three hailing from the High School club). The natural amount of inconvenience was felt by most of the players who essayed the novel rules for the first time, the mysteries of off and

on side and the obligation to leave the hands idle proving almost insurmountable. After some practice no doubt those difficulties will be overcome.[96]

As if to foreshadow the sometimes dubious organisational skills of those running Australian soccer, it is reported that the 'club played without goal posts; as Mr. Briant who had promised to bring them, did not do so, coats were used to mark the goal instead'.[97]

On 7 June the Cricketers met New Town in a competitive inter-club match. 'These clubs met for the return match on Marsh's ground, New Town, on Saturday afternoon, playing the English Association Rules. The result was a draw, no goals being kicked by either side'.[98] The *Tasmanian Mail* also reported on the game, remarking on 'Morriss for the New Town causing special amusement by playing the ball with his head' – possibly the first in a long line of Australian media guffaws about the practice of heading. The writer also complains of the 'absurdity' of the keeper being allowed to throw the ball.[99]

One soccer match in Hobart in 1879 might be a rogue occurrence; two games a month apart intimate a pattern. Moreover, it is reasonable to interpolate 'soccer' practice in-between these dates. However, this was no sparkling beginning of the beautiful game in Australia from which it leapt and bounded, despite the indication that the players intended to keep working at the game. The perceived need for conformity and the weight of numbers ultimately meant the rejection of soccer for the time being.

## CODE CONFUSION

In early 1879 Hobart had no set, singular code of play. Of the four Hobart football clubs, Railway and City insisted on playing under Victorian Rules. New Town had its own code that resembled the Victorian game, though with some important differences, such as a tape between posts under which the ball needed to be kicked to register a goal and the absence of the free kick paid for a mark. As if to add to the complication, the outlying towns and settlements had their own codes as well.

When the City Football Club received an offer of a match from Hotham FC, which is now known as North Melbourne Kangaroos, the club committee decided they could not 'under present circumstances, respond favourably to the offer of the Hotham Club to pay a visit to this colony'.[100] One writer from the *Mercury* lamented the refusal of Hotham's request and suggested 'the formation of an Association [and] uniformity of rules'.[101]

In 1877 when the Tasmanian team Richmond hosted the City club, the reporter remarked, 'It is only fair to say that [City] were at a great disadvantage in having to make the great concession to their opponents of not "running with the ball".'[102] A year later the boot was on the other foot: 'The Richmond team were evidently placed at a disadvantage by the novelty of the mark rule of which they made acquaintance for the first time'.[103]

Some southern Tasmanian codes allowed running with the ball; some did not. Some paid the mark; some did not. Confusion reigned and the home club determined the rules under which the teams would play. Squabbles and protests were the way of things. Tremendous in-fighting also existed among the clubs based on colonial political loyalties. If some footballers, like Boddam, were holding out for the visit of an English football team, others were advocates of the Victorian game.

In late 1878 hopes were still being held for an English visit. A member of the City Club wrote to the *Mercury*: 'Our colony, as compared with the other Australian colonies is but a small one, but, sir, I believe there are sufficient strong and active youths here to form a football association from which we could pick a team worthy to compete with our English friends'. The writer advocated the adoption of a 'general code of rules throughout the colony' that would facilitate footballing commerce with the English.[104] It was felt that such a relationship would lead to other economic and political benefits. The initial adoption of Association Rules by the City Club in early 1879 needs to be seen in this context.

While the promised visit of an English team failed to materialise, the Hotham letter brought home the realisation that extra-colonial football relations were most likely to be established with Victoria and, this being the case, the recently formed Tasmanian Football Association needed to adopt Victorian Rules. In the continued absence of a sign of visiting English teams, those pushing for the 'British' codes had little argument.

One of those leading the charge for Victorian Rules was W H Cundy, who was interviewed by the *Mercury* five decades later in 1931:

When I first came to Tasmania as a youth . . . there was
really no established code. Rugby, soccer, and a sort
of hybrid game were being played, and it can well be
imagined the chaos that existed. I had played what was
then known as the Victorian code in Melbourne . . . but at
first was unable to induce other teams to adopt the Victorian
rules. I had brought over a book of rules, and had 50 copies
printed for distribution, and a meeting was later called at
the old High School, now the University, to discuss the
position. The . . . meeting could not come to a decision to
concentrate on one code, so it was decided that for a season
the teams should play the Victorian rules game, soccer
and Rugby turn about, and at the end of the year decide
which should be adopted, when all were fairly conversant
with the codes. When the vote subsequently was taken, the
Victorian rules won. I believe, by one vote.[105]

A further recollection reported in the *Mercury* on 15 September 1936,
three years after Cundy's death, repeated and reinforced the story:

Few Tasmanians know that the national code of football,
now the predominating code of football in Tasmania,
was introduced to the State by one vote only. Major
W.T. Conder, President of the Australian Amateur
Football Council, told members of the Northern
Tasmanian Football Association last night that when the
late W.H. Cundy came to Tasmania in the 1870s, the
Australian game was not played in Tasmania. The football
played consisted of Soccer, Rugby and a cross between the
two games known as the Tasmanian game. In 1879 those
in control of football in Tasmania decided by one vote to
play what was then known as the Victorian game, and is
now the national game.[106]

Cundy's memories testify to the diversity of Hobart football in early
1879 and the level of disagreement about the way to unify the game
in the colony. Nonetheless, by the end of the 1879 season a modified

version of Victorian Rules was established as the dominant football code in Hobart. Hotham's letter of challenge was central in that process.

Two years later the locals managed to beat the Victorians at their own game, in the process confirming Victorian Rules as the primary winter game in Tasmania. In 1881, with the Victorian Rules in place, Tasmanian football was able to return a belated acceptance of Hotham's challenge. The Hobart game on 5 July was a major event for the southern community. Over 1500 spectators turned out to what the *Mercury* described as 'one of the most exciting games that has ever been played in Tasmania'.[107] The combined southern team overcame a spirited Hotham, by 3 goals to 2.

Despite their victory, the locals knew they had faced a superior foe. The *Mercury* reported that it was 'pleasing to see that our footballers are not too proud to take a lesson in play from a visiting team'. Immediate footballing improvements were noted, especially in relation to 'little marking . . . the smartness of the Victorians in this respect being copied by the local men'.[108]

When Hotham revisited in 1887 the *Launceston Examiner* reminded its readers that the 'visit of the Hotham team about six years ago marked the beginning of a new era in football in this colony'.[109] Generally, their first visit was credited with spreading the gospel of Victorian Rules throughout Tasmania.

## THE VICTORIAN ASCENDANCY

It is worth pausing on three aspects of the ascendancy of Victorian Rules in Hobart in 1879. First, it occurs after a tussle between a British imperialism represented by Boddam and his ilk and the Victorian imperialism of Cundy and the VFA. At this stage the VFA was in a heavily missionary mode, adopting 'an evangelical approach to the advancement of the game', and encouraging its member clubs to play matches 'in provincial areas and beyond'.[110]

The development of Victorian Rules around Australia at this time is not so much an inevitable development 'out of the soil' but a product of patterns of politicised advocacy, evangelism and imposition. The fact that the game was being exported from 'neighbouring' Victoria made it no less a product of cultural imperialism in Tasmania or wherever else it was taken up.

Second, the ascendancy of Victorian rules was not complete. Controversially, the Hobart association kept the crossbar. As the *Mercury* reported on June 16: 'to these (goal) posts shall be attached a horizontal bar, 10ft from the ground, over which the ball must be kicked to secure a goal.' This was a nod to English codes of football and a sign of a residual resistance to the Victorian code. While the crossbar was bolted to the uprights there was still the vain hope of enticing a British team to Tasmania. One correspondent to the *Mercury* felt this decision made 'the so-called adoption of the Victorian code a mockery and a delusion, the innovation being of so glaring a character as to entirely change the form of the play, and to rob it of its principal points of interest'.

> The post of goal keeper, to which one of the coolest and steadiest was ever appointed, and which has been an object of aspiration as a place of trust, is at once swept away, while the occupation of the goal sneak – the quickest, sturdiest, and most alert of the forward players – is also gone.
> The changes consequent on the adoption of this single excrescence from the Rugby Union code are, however, too numerous for noting in detail.[111]

The association executive was accused of being a 'star chamber' that had added this rule after the general meeting had decided to adopt Victorian Rules. And while that seems a fair criticism, this argument had its chance to be ironed out at subsequent meetings.

It is telling that the Hobart footballers kept their crossbar until as late as 1884. In 1883, for example, the association's secretary 'reported that he had written to all the town clubs relative to altering the rules relating to the use of the crossbar and pushing, and had received replies from the whole of them, it being agreed by 136 members to 91 to keep the rules as at present'.[112] In November 1883 the Tasmania delegates to the inter-colonial rules conference held in Melbourne argued for the installation of the crossbar in all colonies. Perhaps surprisingly, according to the *Mercury*, they were defeated by only 9 votes to 6![113]

A third and final point relates to the idea of what game the participants thought they were playing. Had they adopted 'a game of their own'?[114] Were they – reluctantly or otherwise – playing a Victorian colonial imposition? Did they care one way or the other? It is difficult enough to establish the facts, never mind work out what was in the participants' heads – though the following is suggestive.

At the end of the 1879 season a celebratory dinner was held in Hobart on 27 September. The footballers had settled most of their differences and unbeknownst to them were at the beginning of a long historical thread that continues today. The *Mercury* reported a number of speeches given that night:

> Mr. GIBLIN proposed the toast of the evening, 'Success to the Tasmanian Football Association.' (Loud and prolonged cheers.) There was not the least doubt that the game of football had taken such a hold of the young men of Hobart Town that season such as none of them could remember before. (Hear, hear.) It was a grand winter game. Many of them loved cricket with an intense love, but in our climate cricket could not be played all the year round, and there was no game to be compared to the manly old English game of football. (Cheers.)[115]

Giblin, it seems, was fairly confident about the English origins and character of the game in which they were participants. The response suggests that many others agreed with him.

## SOCCER IN THE SHADOWS

After 1879 Association football appears to have retreated into the Hobart background until its re-emergence in 1898 and firm establishment in the early 1900s on the back of migration from the British Isles. The possible continuity of soccer in this period should nonetheless be entertained, even if imagined merely as the informal kicking-around of the remaining surplus round balls that were widely available and sold in the early 1870s.[116]

While those first games of soccer did indeed happen, it is necessary to burrow deep into the historical record to find them. Archivally buried and misremembered, their status as two of the very first games of organised soccer in Australia has been lost. And they remain lost because their discovery has had little purchase, despite the fact that one of them is the first recorded competitive inter-club game of soccer with premiership implications. Curiously, it is not even remembered by those who might be seen to have an interest in doing so, the various soccer governing bodies in Australia.[117] It is barely remembered as just one game of the 1879 Hobart football season, thereby keeping in the shadows the story of the Cricketers' cameo role in the grander narrative of soccer's early Australian rumblings.

The simplistic received history is that Australian Rules (via Melbourne Rules and Victorian Rules) football was played in Hobart from the beginnings of organised football in Tasmania. It is historically inaccurate but remains a culturally powerful truism. It is an error that is repeated and compounded by mythologisers who have their purposes and historians who should know better.

The website 'Tasmania AFL: It's Time', devoted to the ongoing attempt to establish a Tasmanian team in the elite national Australian Rules competition, understandably appeals to ideas of the historical depth of Australian Rules in Tasmania and the state's cultural commitment to the game. It notes that 'Tasmania has a long and proud football history, dating back to the 1860s. Ours was the first state outside of Victoria to play the game, with football clubs established in New Town, Derwent and Stowell in and around 1864'. It happily claims these clubs for Australian Rules, skirting around the historical complications, and asserts:

> A number of clubs came and went and by 1879, the Tasmanian Cricket Association had officially formed a club (called the Cricketers) and Hobart had four senior football teams. Arguments about the rules of the game were solved at a meeting of club secretaries on 12 June, 1879, which formed an association and decided to adopt Victorian Rules with slight modifications.[118]

Given the nature and political project of the organisation making the argument, its use of this shorthand mythology is entirely expected and not particularly unreasonable.

For a professional historian, however, such errors are less forgiveable. Geoffrey Blainey's *A Game of Our Own* is one of the influential and most respected histories of Australian Rules football. Its section on early football in Tasmania, while acknowledging the uncertainty of codes in the colony, nonetheless constructs Melbourne Rules as the norm against which other codes butted. Blainey writes on a football game in Launceston in 1875, intended to be eleven versus eleven but which ended up as eleven versus all-comers:

> This particular match was closer to Rugby than to the football normally played in Melbourne, for the players on various occasions obtained a 'touch down' and with it the right to kick for goal. Four years later football in Launceston, unmistakeably, was played according to the Australian rules.[119]

Rhetorically, Blainey presents the Launceston game as a departure from the norm. Despite quibbles that could be made about the fact that 'touch downs' were performed in many forms of football other than Rugby and that the 'Australian Rules' did not exist in 1879, the important error here is the inadvertent deception of constructing Tasmanian football as Victorian Rules *in embryo*. This is compounded by an illustrating photograph, anachronistically representing the post-ascendancy southern Tasmanian football team from 1890 (with its characteristic sleeveless playing vests, bulging biceps and brimming confidence) as a pictorial example of a moment 11 years earlier when Tasmanian football was in disarray. Blainey's subsequent reference to Tasmanian football is to Hotham's visit in 1881 – when the code war is over and Victorian Rules is established as the Tasmanian winter game.

Most amateur and professional historians allow for the fact that much of the football played around Australia in the 1850s and 1860s was often an undifferentiated and usually locally 'flexible' set of behaviours. Many, however, are in error because they fail properly to trace the shift to codification. Sometimes a convenient look-away allows Australian Rules to be there in place smiling innocently when the historian returns to the narrative. Almost all amateur histories do this; as do some professional accounts. Series of tussles, arguments and code wars get effaced in this process, whereby competing codes and claims are written out of the narrative.

David Young, the author of *Sporting Island: A History of Sport and Recreation in Tasmania*, commits this kind of error. Despite the momentary formal adoption of Association rules in 1879, which Young acknowledges, soccer is only 'introduced'[120] (like a species foreign to Tasmania) in the late 1890s, whereas Australian Rules 'rises'[121] (like a tree from the soil). The indexing convention adopted for the book also embeds a particular narrative. Soccer and the rugby codes are given their own entries, whereas Australian Rules sits within the generic entry on football (alongside all references to pre-codified forms of the game).

The same kind of flaw applies to many of the histories of Melbourne football, with some notable exceptions. Other codes are excluded from historical consideration by the invention of a great Australian Rules tradition which, having acknowledged (or asserted) its contemporary social dominance, looks back over history and colonises the lot for itself.[122] The circular logic runs: if there's a reference to a game of football in a Melbourne newspaper in the 1850s then it must be to Australian Rules football because all football games in colonial Victoria lead inevitably to present-day Australian Rules.[123]

The better historians attack this kind of logic head-on. They are very careful to argue that the game inaugurated by Wills and his fellows in 1858 is an English game introduced to the colony and not some inevitable genealogical progression from pre-existing games. They point out that 'Wills and others made it known in the press that they had introduced a new code of football into the colony – not that they had adopted and reshaped a game that was already in existence'.[124] The Australian-Rules-*in-embryo* argument is ruled out by this reasoning. The early games resembled the Melbourne Rules to come, but they also had many differences.

Soccer historians also need to take this argument on board. It would be ahistorical to look for organised soccer prior to the game's codification in England in 1863. Yet attentive historians nonetheless need to keep their eyes and minds open for games resembling soccer being played well back in Australian history. Football resembling Association football rather than what became Australian Rules was regularly played in mid-century Melbourne and later.[125] Hobart's New Town FC, an earlier incarnation of present-day Glenorchy Magpies [Australian Rules] FC, played soccer before they played Australian Rules.

But these foundation narratives are hegemonic and soccer counter-narratives are rarely taken seriously. Because of this entrenchment it is not just a simple matter of correcting foundation errors and allowing the truth to unfold. Like fallen boulders that have caused the damming of a creek and the removal of which has no consequence once the dam is established, their consequences need to be dismantled and unravelled. Such errors have been a deep impediment to attempts to write other histories.

When Chris Hudson came to compile his comprehensive history of soccer in Tasmania, *A Century of Soccer, 1898–1998*, he began with the claim that 'British Association Football first came to Australia in 1880'.[126] He repeats the three intertwined myths: soccer's late importation; Australia's soccer origins in Sydney; and Australian Rules' Tasmanian universality. Guided and blinded by these narratives, Hudson inadvertently ignores a crucial part of his own state's history. This is no slight on Hudson. At the time of his research, the corrective documents were buried in the archive and hard to find. And it would have required a willful disregard of, and resistance to, the established narratives to allow him to look for a game so early on.[127]

On the other hand, fortune might have smiled upon him. Had Hudson been aware that southern Tasmania only just adopted Victorian Rules football by one single vote in 1879, his project would have been altered fundamentally. And had Hudson found James Sprent's letter to the *Mercury* on 3 July 1926, it would have caused a major re-conceptualisation of both the content and the method of his study:

> 'Referee' states that Soccer was first started in Tasmania by the late Mr. J.B.B. Honeysett in 1912. Re-started would be more correct, as the game was played regularly in Hobart during 1900, 1901 and 1902. Australian Football in this State being under a cloud at the time several old Soccer players combined to introduce the game, and the chief credit must be given to the Rev. F. Taylor, of Holy Trinity, now of Longford. He had played for Durham University, and had, I think, captained the team. Rev. H.H. Anderson, of Hutchins School, was another old player: in fact, the first practice was held on his ground. T.F. Hills, of Friends' School, a gigantic centre forward had also played in good

company at Home. Three teams were formed, University,
Gunners, and Sandy Bay, the two latter being from the
volunteers. Regular matches were played for three years,
and if the skill of the new recruits was not great, we
nevertheless had a lot of fun. Later the Australian game
regained its popularity, chiefly owing to the efforts of the
late W.H. Gill, and the University declared for the old
game again. So for a while Soccer was neglected. But if
'Referee' cares to do a bit of research work as to the origin
of the game in Tasmania I can give him the address of an
old friend, who swears that a round-ball game was played
regularly on the Domain over 50 years ago.[128]

Sprent's letter intimates an important point: the latent potential of
soccer rapidly to move into spaces vacated by dominant codes when
they make way, either voluntarily or reluctantly. It is not known whether
'Referee' ever got around to visiting the 'old friend'. In all likelihood
his stories died with him. But if Sprent was correct soccer was played in
Hobart in 1876 or earlier.

The following reflection from 1876 relates to a particularly violent
game of football in Hobart, one that created a deal of public rancour
and press correspondence. The game was probably not soccer, but the
response seems to be a clear expression of one individual's impulse
towards the kicking game:

SIR, - I am a Lancashire man, but to be more precise in
locality 'a Bolton Felly.' Any townsman of my age cannot
but remember the seven clog shin kicks (or purring)
of those days. The opposing sides generally kicked in
Bradshawgate or Church gate. It was a warfare of English
v. French, and football has long to be remembered by those
engaged in, I may say, these Waterloo contests.

At a match like this, which includes legs and arms and
objectionable exclamations, temper is hard to keep. The
recent contest in Hobart Town between the City and New
Norfolk Clubs, calls up to memory the scenes I witnessed
half a century ago; but without a bias, I would recommend

to all clubs, more of the feet and less of the fists and jaw.

Yours truly.
BOLTON FELLY.
August 5th.[129]

Do Sprent and 'Bolton Felly' point to a soccerite sensibility of long residence in Tasmania and, by extension, Australia? It is a vital question because an affirmative answer explodes a number of origin myths.

## BRISBANE, 1875

It is not necessary to speculate about cultural silences and faint archival traces to assert that the Sydney-origins thesis has been dismantled. But nor will it do to replace the Sydney thesis with an earlier Hobart variation. The Hobart Cricketers' two matches were not the first games of soccer (codified or otherwise) in Australia. A number of earlier games were also played.

One took place on Saturday 7 August 1875 in Woogaroo (now Goodna) just outside of Brisbane. The *Queenslander* reported that Brisbane FC met the inmates and warders of the Woogaroo Lunatic Asylum on the football field in the grounds of the Asylum, with a rule 'that the ball should not be handled nor carried'[130] and which Thomas Power in the Victorian publication *The Footballer* claimed was played under 'Association rules'.[131]

A fascinating story is waiting to be told about why the Woogaroo Asylum played soccer when all other clubs in the region seemed to playing Rugby or a Queensland variation on the Melbourne Rules.[132] It may well have boiled down to the preference of the Asylum's superintendent, John Jaap, or even the players themselves.[133] Jaap was the superintendent of the Asylum between 1872 and his death at 39 years in 1877. He graduated from Glasgow University in 1858 with an MD and was married in London in 1869. In January 1871 he was living and working as a doctor in Warwick, in south-east Queensland, prior to taking up the post at Woogaroo.[134]

Jaap was noted for implementing humane methods and programs at the Woogaroo institution. He 'employed patient labour to establish a piggery and farm pursuits, which were a feature of the asylum for many years. [He] drew attention to the overcrowded conditions at the asylum, a perennial problem which plagued the institution for most of its existence'.[135] He also supervised the implementation of a sports program.[136]

Football can be seen as part of a continuum of 'improving' activities established by Jaap, who would likely have been in favour of Association rules, given that he learned his organised football at Glasgow University. The game there was described as 'a dribbling one' in which:

> the ball must be kicked and could not be carried or handled, no collaring or hacking was permitted and there was little rough play. If the ball was caught in the air a free, that is an undisturbed, kick was allowed. The player who held the ball dropped it from his hand and kicked it as [it] fell. The game was practically the same as Hand Ball as regards numbers and manner of playing; in the one case the ball was struck with the hand and the other with the foot.[137]

There were at least two other games of football under Jaap's supervision, an earlier one against Brisbane FC on 19 July 1873 and one against Rangers FC on 24 June 1876, though there is no indication of the rules used in those games. Were the 1873 game found to have been played under Association rules (as might have been the case under Jaap's direction) it would be the earliest codified game *on record* in Australia.

But nor would this be the very first game of soccer in Australia. There is little doubt that there were earlier games, less formal, less structured perhaps, and which escaped the notice of the press.

The nearly disabling problem for this kind of research is that as researchers venture archivally backward in time the images become more blurred and the distinctions among codes become harder to make. Even as potential origin points become temporally closer they recede into the shadows of archival absence. In private correspondence with Gavin Kitching, Tony Collins makes the vital point that 'almost all historians of "football" look at history through a teleological lens, projecting current concerns and configurations backwards onto the past. At its simplest level this can be found in the assumption that "football" is a synonym for their favoured modern code of football'.[138]

Yet the dilemma for football historians lies in the necessity of engagement with the established origins that lie at the heart of the professional and amateur historiography of all major sports, origins that both orient and limit debate. Moreover, present-day administrators compound the problem by using anniversaries of origin to generate publicity. They help to get stories rolling: 'Once upon a time Wills or Webb Ellis or Doubleday did something so special that they got a great game started'. Aside from often being simply incorrect, origin theses tend to nurture hegemonic narratives that by their very nature rule counter-narratives out of bounds.

# CHAPTER 3

# THE FOREIGN GAME IN MELBOURNE

The period of soccer's first organisation in Victoria (the 1880s) is sometimes referred to as 'Marvellous Melbourne', a time of boom and inward migration following a twenty-year slump. This boom lasted about a decade and then collapsed, flattening much social and cultural life in the process. Over the 50-year period between 1860 and 1910, Victoria's net immigration was close to zero, as was soccer's effective progress.

Soccer initially found a muffled welcome in Melbourne. Yet even as it was elbowing some room for itself in the 1880s it was losing the battle of representation. From early silence through moments of vague dismissal and gentle ridicule to periods of sustained unacknowledgement and forgetting, soccer rarely received fair representation in the Victorian press until well after its reformation in 1908.

Victoria is the perfect case study for this marginalisation of soccer because historically it has been the state in which the game has found the least welcome – though it is not necessarily the state where it found the most soccerphobic reaction. In the period before the First World War the press in Western Australia, South Australia and Tasmania allowed correspondence that was often more rebarbative than its Victorian equivalents. Soccer was seen as much worse than a mere feeble foreign presence. It was the suspicious excess baggage of the 'new' Australian.

## 1863–1883 SOCCER: THE GAME YET TO HAPPEN

It seems incongruous that a game whose development is at least acknowledged in almost every British colony in the 1870s should be so badly ignored in Victoria. The sporadic advocacies aside, the Melbourne press fails to mention the game domestically. It rarely, if ever, reports on the game as *Association* football as it is played in Britain in the 1870s and fails to report on the game as it is played in Sydney (between 1880 and 1883). This could be put down to misidentification, ignorance, lack of interest, or, perhaps in a more paranoid mode, a kind of social engineering whereby the game is deliberately given as little oxygen as possible.

While organised soccer is not being played or reported, a game very much like it is – Victorian Rules football. As has been noted above, widespread confusion abounded about the similarities and differences between the games. One possibility is that the use of the name 'Association' football around Australia tended to generate uncertainty, referring to either soccer or Victorian Rules depending on time or place.[139] Sometimes that similarity arose from observation. In 1878 the *Sydney Morning Herald* manages to compose the following sentence, equating Victorian and English Association rules:

> The contest was arranged, primarily, with the object of
> giving that section of the public who take an interest in this
> winter pastime an opportunity of contrasting the *Victorian,
> or more properly speaking, English Association game*, with the
> Rugby.[140] [emphasis added]

Does this false equation have validity across the colonial border in Victoria? Does the fact that both games are sometimes seen as forms of anti-Rugby with arguable Harrow/Cambridge lineages allow them to be equated in the Melbourne press of the 1870s? It is entirely feasible that an English or Scottish migrant who came to Victoria as a 'soccer man' in the 1870s could have found himself able to adapt relatively easily to Victorian Rules whereas the same migrant to Sydney had a more difficult adaptation and an earlier encouragement to form a Football Association.[141] Does it only become 'necessary' for British Association rules to emerge for the ground-based round-ball footballers in Melbourne when Victorian Rules diverges from its original parameters and allows players to take the ball up from the ground by hand, thereby removing that last vestige of technical similarity between Victorian and Association rules?

Would this putative individual transitioning from soccer to Australian Rules thereby lead Victorians to assume an equivalence between their game and the one growing in popularity in England? On the rare moments when soccer is reported from Britain, usually the international games between England and Scotland, it is simply noted as football. A possible reciprocal misidentification is occurring simultaneously in Britain where it is reported that Association football is growing in Melbourne often without any reference to its difference from British Association football.[142]

This argument is likely fanciful, but it does get to the point that Australian Rules and Association football have engaged in an intimate dance in Melbourne for nearly 150 years. Virtually identical in genetic terms, the games have actively denied this kinship since the moment they came face to face as mature games in 1883. Like distant brothers who grew up in different physical and cultural environments, they have in the course of life come to dislike and distrust each other, not truly understanding the depth of their kinship. In this reading soccer is not so much the menacing invader but is more the 'parasitic twin', or the wicked ghost that has haunted the mansion of Melbourne football since before it was even built.

One commentator in the mid-1860s went as far as suggesting that the Melbourne and Association rules were more or less identical when the English FA rules were laid down. 'Free Kick' writes:

> The Football Association was accordingly formed, and a set of rules drawn up, which by a very curious coincidence, are very nearly similar to those which were decided on at a meeting of representatives of football clubs, held at the Parade Hotel, near Melbourne, some 5 years ago. I forget exactly at this time who were the gentlemen appointed but amongst them I know were Mr J B Thompson, Mr Smith, then of the Scotch College, Mr Hammersley, Mr Wills, Mr Wray and others, and it is certainly creditable in every way to the judgment of the gentlemen then appointed, that the very rules they then decided on have subsequently been adopted by the members of the Football Association in England. Whether a stray copy (for the rules were neatly printed and got up) ever found its way home I do not know, but if not it is a strong argument in favour of our own code, that the football parliaments

assembled on opposite sides of the globe, should bring the identical same result of their labours.[143]

An extraordinary suggestion has been made by one historian that the Melbourne Rules could well have been influenced directly by the Sheffield Rules via Henry Creswick, thereby drawing an even closer relationship between soccer and Australian Rules.[144]

'Free Kick' goes on to emphasise that the mark and the resulting free kick are a point of difference and two of the more exciting aspects of the Melbourne Rules:

> Some persons have objected to the ball being caught,
> and the consequent free kick, but I cannot see any great
> objection to it. It makes the players on each side smarter
> when the ball is near either goal, it causes a variety in the
> game, gives every now and then a short spell, which many
> who have been running hard are very glad of; and when
> the kick is made, the ball generally takes an upward course,
> thereby ensuring that most enlivening scene, a charge on
> both sides to get first catch or kick at the falling ball.[145]

It is important to note that the phenomenon of the mark and set shot for goal happens 'now and then' and is a special moment in Melbourne Rules as described above. Nowhere in this passage is the anachronistic and oft-made spectacular 'high mark' that others have observed. Using 'Free Kick' as their evidence, historians falsely argue that the 'high mark' was 'already part of the game'[146] when the excitement is in the massed charge and not the individual leap. They are guilty of transferring their own contemporary vision of the game's excitement onto its earliest days.[147]

In any case, the urge to see the mark as representing a substantial departure from other codes should be resisted. In 1864 catching the ball is permitted under Association rules and almost all of the English public-school games. English Rugby League historian Tony Collins points to 'the commonplace' nature of the mark: 'Commonly known as a "fair catch", the rule allowed a player who caught the ball cleanly before it touched the ground to claim a "free kick", the right to kick the ball unimpeded by his opponents'. Collins notes that C W Alcock's *Football Annual* in 1868 outlined the 'widespread use of this rule':

At Harrow, Rugby, Winchester, Marlborough, Cheltenham, Uppingham, Charterhouse, Westminster, Haileybury, Shrewsbury [public schools], Football Association, Sheffield Association and Brighton [College], catching is allowed, but at Eton, Rossall and Cambridge the ball must not be touched with the hands.[148]

Given that catching the ball is a legitimate practice in the great majority of the contemporary codes of football, who is making the objections observed by 'Free Kick'? What code or kind of football do they represent? Are they advocates of Eton, Rossall and Cambridge or do they represent some other un-named footballing faction, one that represents a soccerite impulse?

The standard fare of Melbourne FC rules was ground kicking and scrimmages. This is acknowledged by many histories of Australian Rules.[149] A poem published in 1858 in *Melbourne Punch*, simply entitled 'Football', also attests to this. In over 100 lines it refers directly to kicking at least a dozen times and feet, shins and calves at least a dozen more. Not once is the ball represented as being carried or marked. The ball disappears into scrimmages and only rarely escapes to soar through the air before being brought to earth once more. The following lines capture the tenor of the poem and perhaps the essential quality of Melbourne football at the time:

> And now the kicking fun begins,
> The battle of the toes and shins;
> Down went the ball, and, crushing thick,
> The strife was great for primal kick,
> Long scuffled then the blue and motley,
> Long waged the battle fierce and hotly;
> The patience of a very Job
> Was tired to get that leather globe,
> Well free from strife of blow and bru'se,
> And wilderness of boots and shoes.[150]

The famous image 'Football in Yarra Park 1874' by Melbourne wood-engraver Samuel Calvert allows a similar point to be made about the ground-based nature of the game. While one player is looking to

'Football in Yarra Park 1874' by Samuel Calvert, 13 July 1874.
Courtesy of the State Library of Victoria.

handle or catch the ball, he is peripheral to the action; he may also be a goalkeeper. The image seems more appropriate to a soccer-like game than it is to Australian Rules. It has been argued that such images are derivative or copied from English sources and are therefore unreliable representations. However, this engraving was domestically produced. It seems to represent actual people and has, like the poem cited above, greater claims to authenticity.[151]

As late as 1879 *The Footballer* (published in Carlton as a compendium/almanac of Melbourne football) emphasised ground kicking, and warned players against playing the ball with the hand when a kick was an option. Most remarkable, however, is the advocacy of the practice of 'Rushing *alias* Sniggling' in which a player was instructed to:

> Run gently forward, patting the ball before you with either foot, as occasions serve, taking care never to let the ball get above a few yards in front of you. Gradually increase your speed till you can keep the ball well under control without impairing your rate of progression. This is very difficult of attainment, but it is of invaluable service in actual play. In

this way a good player will take the ball through a whole
host of his enemies, outspeeding this one, eluding that,
until he gets a favorable chance at goal.[152]

These instructions are simply not applicable to the game of Australian
Rules, or to the Victorian Rules in 1879, as history constructs it. The
instructions are more appropriate to the practice of dribbling in a round-
ball, soccer-like game or in a rugby mode focused on the dribbling
method. This, and the text's lack of focus on the mark, suggests that
this material has been lifted from an instruction manual for Association
football.[153] One alternative is that this material was actually useful for the
crack footballers of Carlton, Essendon, Geelong, Hotham and company.
And if this is the case some major revisions of Australian Rules history
are urgently required.

## 1883: A HARD WELCOME

On 6 April 1883 the *Argus* first acknowledged Association football being
played in Melbourne. Even while the game is described as 'awkward'
and 'tame' without many 'skilful manipulations' or 'excitements', a
nonetheless positive and cautiously welcoming tone is adopted. 'As
advertised, the scratch match under the British rules took place on
Saturday last [March 31], in the old Civil Service Football Ground',
read the report. It went on:

> There were about 25 players on the ground, besides a good
> many spectators, most of whom seemed to understand the
> game. It appeared rather awkward to some of the players,
> especially those who have been used to the Victorian game,
> as the rules are altogether different, but after a little practise
> it is the intention of the club to give the game a fair test
> before the Melbourne public. The game is 'football pure
> and simple'.[154]

On 7 May a correspondent from *The Australasian Sketcher with Pen
and Pencil* also mentioned the first machinations of organised soccer in
Melbourne. He might also be credited with the first example of bad-

faith soccer writing in Melbourne, insofar as he describes soccer as an imported and therefore doomed game. 'In connexion with football,' he wrote, 'an attempt is being made to introduce the English Association game, but as the popularity of the game as played here has long been established, the effort can only end in failure.'[155]

This was no hearty welcome. As the *Argus* explained critically after seeing the first inter-colonial game played in Melbourne on Thursday 16 August, 1883:

> The main principle of the game is that with the exception of the goalkeeper on either side, no player is permitted to handle either the ball or his opponents, although he may butt the ball in an inelegant way with his head. The drop-kicking and marking, together with the skilful system of exchanging little marks that have so popularised the Victorian game, are entirely wanting . . . About 200 people witnessed the match.[156]

A reporter for the *Age* was similarly bemused by the practice of heading, adding that the rules of the game implied 'physical degeneracy on the part of a community which plays it'.[157]

After watching the second game, the *Argus* seemed to agree with the *Age*.

> The English game bears about the same relation to the Victorian game that bowls does to cricket. It is not nearly so rough as the Victorian pastime, nor so exciting to the spectator; but on the other hand, the tactics are far less likely to provoke ill feeling and deliberate ill-usage.[158]

Yet this criticism contradicted the position adopted three days earlier. After the first match, the *Argus* saw a kind of violence missed by the *Age*:

> If the game is apparently less rough to an observer, the element of danger is not wanting, and when a number of players come together, all kicking at the ball, some nasty bruises are received. A spiteful player has also a chance of seriously injuring an opponent without his motives being

suspected – a thing which could scarcely happen under the Victorian rules.[159]

In another formulation that rings down the ages, soccer players are constructed as simultaneously cowardly and violent, wanting to inflict damage without detection or responsibility.[160] Just in case readers had not received the message, in August the *Argus* reported that the matches had been 'decided failures' and that there was 'no chance whatever of the English game being popularised in this colony.'[161]

And so, in the first few months of soccer's reception in Melbourne, it was described in turn as tame, unexciting, degenerate, soft, vaguely ludicrous and awkward, a facilitator of cowardly and unmanly violence, unestablished, not as good as Australian Rules, a decided failure, and peopled by imports – notions that riffle through the history of sports commentary in Australia.

The *South Australian Register* soon echoed the derision of the *Argus* and the *Age*, arguing that the inter-colonial Association Rules match between New South Wales and Victoria 'did not excite any interest' and that 'our Australian game has taken too firm a root to be affected by an inferior style of play'.[162]

It was a tough southern welcome, one that at least had the advantage of preparing aficionados for a long future of derogation.[163] Yet the hard welcome seemed quickly to soften. Reports over the next three decades are generally minimal, understated and uncritical, sometimes positive, though often absent. Rarely does the game come in for outright derision; it is almost as if, with the warning shots fired, the job of slotting the game into its place has been performed. If some within the Victorian community, with an eye on the growing crowds in Britain, had feared a soccer takeover, the fact that none was forthcoming enabled them to relax.

The Englishness or Britishness of the game, often mentioned in newspaper reportage, was a feature the participants were also keen to emphasise. Such claims to being a British or Empire code of football have often been assumed to be the aspect that differentiates soccer from Australian Rules and even Rugby League, which are seen to be domestic games. Rugby League historian Tony Collins believes this should be taken with a grain of salt. He claims that 'the culture of Australian Rules was firmly British':

Its terms of reference were entirely within a British,
Muscular Christian framework. Thus the motto on the
masthead of the house organ of the Victorian Football
League (VFL), the *Football Record*, first published in 1912,
was the unashamedly British 'Fair Play is Bonnie Play'.
Nor, despite the significant Irish presence in Victoria, was
the VFL the slightest bit hesitant in its monarchism …
These sentiments were not merely for public consumption.
Internally, the leadership of Australian Rules resorted to
British values and principles in organizational debates.
Thus, when in 1911 a dispute broke out between the South
Australian National Football League and the Australasian
Football Council, Charles Brownlow of the AFC defended
his position by saying that 'it was only British fair play to
hear both sides of the question'.[164]

Australian Rules wanted two bob each way on this question because,
while it asserted its Britishness, it also wanted to claim a uniquely
Australian identity. Collins suggests that Australian Rules was British
when it came to matters of Empire and Australian when it came to
internal Australian football and cultural politics.

Of course, the sport promoted itself as uniquely Australian,
not least when contrasting itself to other codes of football.
But this was not counterposed to being British. Like cricket
in Yorkshire or rugby union in Cornwall, the promotion of
a strong regional identity that thought itself superior to the
metropolitan centre did not threaten, nor seek to threaten,
its essential underlying Britishness.[165]

The more pertinent point is that the soccer players, the Anglo-Association
footballers, probably saw their game as a way to connect *with* rather than
assert a difference *from* 'home', and a product of this subtle differentiation
– a refusal of belonging – may well be one of the great assumed cultural
weaknesses passed down to the inheritors of the code.

## 1884–1895: ACKNOWLEDGEMENT WITHOUT ASPERSION

After the initial dismissal and gentle ridicule in 1883, the press shifted to a mode of acknowledgement without aspersion. Yet even while the coverage was mildly supportive, three dissonant harmonics were struck at regular intervals: peculiarity, unpopularity, Britishness.

Through 1884 the *Argus* reports were generally favourable without being either extensive or effusive – though the report on the final of the George and George Cup captures the sense of triumph and achievement for the Richmond team in a 'fast and exciting' contest.[166] And despite the initial attempt to create the impression that soccer is a game without physical risk, injuries *were* reported: 'During the football match, under the Anglo-Australian Association rules, between Carlton and South Melbourne on Saturday, Drew, a player in the latter side, broke his arm'.[167]

The game received coverage in the post-season period when a proposed tour to England is mentioned. The game's connection with and the participants' orientation towards England was made clear.

This quietly positive press continued into 1885. The increase from four to six clubs was noted and good crowds were sometimes acknowledged.[168] A game between South Melbourne and Prahran was conducted 'in the presence of a goodly number of spectators, who appeared to enjoy the peculiarities of this game'.[169] Again the peculiarities are mentioned, while the following report managed to chime with all the discordant notes:

> A match was played on Saturday afternoon at the Richmond Cricket ground, between the New South Wales eleven and the team selected from those Victorian and English players who follow the rules of the Anglo-Australian football Association. In consequence of the principles of the game not being well understood, and the counter attractions elsewhere, the attendance was very small – not more than 200 or 300 persons being present.[170]

These attitudes continued into 1886. The phrase, 'fast and exciting game' entrenched itself as a staple of match reports. In May, 'Carlton won a good and decidedly fast game' against Prahran.[171] And soccer's reputation as the 'novelty' game was further enhanced by the introduction of four-a-side football to the Caledonian Society of Melbourne's annual sports carnival in May:

> A novelty was introduced by the supporters of the British Association game of football who mustered teams of four men each of the Prahran, South Melbourne, Richmond, and Carlton clubs to play in heats of 10 minutes each for a six guinea trophy. The game, which was umpired by Mr H. Parkinson was won by the Prahran Club by one touch down against Carlton.[172]

It is possible that the description of the scoring method is a mistake, though it is not out of the question that 'touch downs' could be used in this small-sided version of soccer, drawing on a variant of public-school rules.

The volume of soccer reporting increased in 1887 in keeping with what appears to be a gradual expansion of the game – though this may merely be an impression created by the increased press coverage. It was reported on 3 May that a match 'was played on Saturday afternoon last on the Scotch College cricket ground. The teams consisted chiefly of players from clubs in the old country'.[173] The brief yet generally positive commentary followed through the year. The 'strangeness' of the game was reiterated and some substantial reports were published, especially in relation to the inter-colonial games with New South Wales (the final one of which represents the first-ever full-scale soccer match at the Melbourne Cricket Ground (MCG)).[174] This game's status as the first at such a vital meeting place of Australian sport is obliterated by the MCG Trust's claim that the 'first known soccer (or "football") match played at the MCG was between Victoria and Tasmania on July 17, 1912'.[175] Like so many other ostensibly innocent and inadvertent historiographical/archival errors, this one also facilitates a powerful disruption to the game's belonging in Australia.

Soccer reports began to thin out in 1888. The *Argus* seemed to reduce its commentary even as the Melbourne game is being noticed further afield. The *Portland Guardian* reported at the foot of its football column on 14 May: 'Carlton v. South Melbourne – Carlton 3 goals (one disputed), South Melbourne 2 goals. This match was for Messrs George and Georges' Challenge Cup, and was played under the British Association Rules'.[176] The *South Australian Register* notes on 11 June that the Melbourne 'Rovers met the South Melbourne under the British

Association rules. The Souths gained 6 goals and the Rovers 2 goals'. It was put, however, in stark contrast with the '20,000 spectators' at 'the [Victorian Rules] match of Carlton v. Geelong'.[177] In August the *South Australian Register* reported on Carlton's win over Melbourne Rovers.[178]

While press coverage of soccer seemed to be fading, the on-field quality was not diminished. The *Argus* reported that both Carlton and Melbourne Rovers put 'strong teams on the field' with Carlton winning 4–1 and thereby claiming the George and George Challenge Cup.[179] It also noted three days later that the Victorian team was selected from five clubs.[180] This team toured New South Wales in July 1888, losing 5–2 to the miners of Joadja, near Mittagong, before twice defeating New South Wales.[181]

From 1889 the reporting of soccer in Melbourne was sporadic. With a three-team competition consisting of Carlton, South Melbourne and Melbourne Rovers, the game was on the wane.

There were few local soccer reports from 1890, and the main soccer focus of 1891 was on the alleged theft of the George and George and Beaney cups:

> At the City Court yesterday, Robert Amson, formerly a
> member of the Carlton Football Club playing the British
> Association game of football was charged with the larceny
> as a bailee of two silver cups, valued at £65, the property of
> Mr W.K Spence and other members of the British Football
> Association of Victoria. Mr Panton P.M., presided and Mr
> Gillott appeared to defend the accused. The offence alleged
> against Amson was that as captain of the Carlton Club
> which won the cups in competitions during 1888 and the
> two following years he took charge of them, and on the 1st
> of April, 1890, pawned them at Magner's pawnshop in King
> street, for £7 10s. The cups which were presented to the
> association by Messrs George and George and Dr Beaney
> were not released by Amson, but were subsequently sold
> at auction and bought for £10 by a Mr Lewis of Broken
> Hill. The Bench, having heard the evidence committed the
> accused to stand his trial at the Central Criminal Court on
> the 10th inst. Bail was allowed in one surety of £10.[182]

Amson was eventually found not guilty.[183]

In 1892 the only reference to soccer was that Australian Rules players were resorting to the use of British Association tactics. 'While the rain continued,' reported the *Argus*, 'there was always a crowd of players on the ball, and a good deal of British Association play and miskicks.'[184]

This is one of the earliest references to 'soccer tactics' being used in Australian Rules. It figures soccer as a game played in a degraded situation, a lesser game to which the players resort in wet or muddy conditions. But it also acknowledges the kinship between the codes where in certain circumstances they come to resemble each other once more.

Soccer tactics were again employed in a game between Melbourne and Geelong on 27 June 1894. The *Argus* reported that players 'were for the most part content to play the association game, and kick the ball without handling it'.[185] Immediately below this report was a notice advertising a meeting 'of footballers playing under . . . the British Association rules' and in July 1894 an effort was made to get soccer going again. A scratch match was organised at Middle Park in South Melbourne.[186]

By August the first in a crucially important genre of Australian soccer letters was published, that which mistakenly identifies the regeneration of soccer in Australia as a founding moment. 'By your yesterday's issue I perceive that British Association football has been introduced into this colony,' wrote 'Old County Player' to the *Argus*. 'Would the hon. secretary of the newly formed club kindly publish his name and address, so that those wishing to join (I among the number) might know with whom to communicate?'[187] It is a genre that obliterates history even as it brings attention to the 'now' and recurs in various forms with telling impact throughout Australia over the next 120 years.

The secretary of the British Association Football Club responded to 'Old County Player' but did not correct his error that soccer had been 'introduced to this colony'.

On 6 August 1894 Middle Park was again host to a soccer match, this time between HMS *Katoomba* and the Combined British Association Teams. The combined team won 7–1 in a 'fast and exciting game' played before 1000 spectators.[188] On 15 August notice was given of a general meeting of the association to 'be held at Young and Jackson's to-morrow, when new members and old are requested to attend'.[189] The purpose might well have been to organise the 'annual' England versus Scotland game which took place at Middle Park on 1 September.[190]

Practice, scratch, naval and 'married versus single' matches were the meagre staple of 1895 before a new competition emerged. Yarraville Wanderers beat Prahran in the semi-final and defeated Melbourne in the final of the Hamilton Cup on 31 August. 'The final match in the Hamilton Cup competition was played on Saturday and after a most exciting game resulted in a victory for the Wanderers by 3 goals to nil,' reported the *Argus*.[191]

By 1896 the organised game had waned. A meeting of the 'Victorian British Association Football Union' was to be held 'at the Clarence Hotel, opposite the General post-office' on 11 August 1896'.[192] It is hard to work out whether this is just one more aborted soccer association or a Rugby organisation misnamed by the *Argus*. Either way it matters little. From this point onwards Victorian soccer is historiographically dead for more than a decade with only rare extrinsic naval games to fly the soccer flag.

Before 1896 was out, however, there was another reference to 'British Association tactics', in the Geelong versus Carlton game in August. This game was one of the watershed moments in the evolution of Australian Rules. Geelong utterly dominated proceedings yet they had to share the points. Not long after this behinds were included as part of the scoring system in Australian Rules football.

The idea of Australian Rules footballers using 'Association tactics', in kicking off the ground in certain conditions, has been noted. However, this report from the *Argus* refers to a change in the system of play in which the players gave up trying to mark and carry the ball and kicked it off the ground for most of the game – in many ways a return to the older form of Victorian Rules football played prior to the 1880s:

> Geelong and Carlton had a fast game on the MCC
> ground, because both sides determined to play the British
> Association game – no handling – as soon as the rain came,
> and it was marvellous to see the ball sliding and shooting
> everywhere as delusive as a greasy pig, with the bulk of the
> players apparently never able to catch up to it, although the
> whole 40 were at times trying to do so. The first quarter
> was fairly even and fast, but in the second Geelong had a
> good deal the best of it and scored their only goal. Carlton
> getting their solitary one in the last quarter. A goal apiece

made it a draw, with every appearance of a good game,
until you glance at the behinds column, and note that
Geelong scored 13 behinds to 1, and had very bad luck
indeed in having to share the points when having so much
the best of the field work. Taking it all through they had 19
shots for goal and Carlton 4.[193]

This was the moment when Australian Rules officials, frustrated with low-scoring draws, engineered a significant rule change that altered the game fundamentally. This particular report reads, anachronistically, like a present-day soccer report bemoaning the utter statistical dominance of one team in a game they failed to win. Interestingly, the reported game was considered fast *because* of the adoption of soccer tactics, hinting at a yearning on the writer's part for something like the absent game of soccer.

Yet it would take another seven years before soccer was reported on again in Melbourne, and until 1908 for another serious attempt to reconstitute the game in a state now firmly in the grip of Australian Rules football. It had been a long 24 years, first in shadow and then in gloomy dark. A foreign game, indeed.

# CHAPTER 4

# THE CALM AND THE STORM

The gradual rise of soccer in regions around Australia during the 1890s and 1900s coincided with the game's hiatus in Melbourne. 'Years ago the game had a fair hold in Victoria,' noted the *West Australian* in 1904, 'but when bad times came along, most of the players migrated and some of them have since helped to introduce the game to the youth of this State.'[194]

This observation points to a dispersal, if not a diaspora, of soccer players and supporters from Melbourne in a time of economic downturn. A E Gibbs, a central figure in the Anglo-Australian Football Association in Melbourne, returned to New Zealand in 1890 and immediately re-involved himself in the game there, eventually taking on national executive roles and representing the New Zealand Football Association to the FA.[195] Soccer in Coraki in northern New South Wales received a great impetus from Dr Opie, an ex-Victorian representative player who left Melbourne after 1908.[196] Towns and cities in Tasmania and South Australia also experienced a surge of soccer in this period, as did Mildura on the South Australian–Victorian border.

## PERTH AND MELBOURNE BEFORE THE FIRST WORLD WAR

The goldfields of Western Australia attracted a number of Melbournians and, seemingly, most of its soccer players. 'Spectator' also made the intriguing suggestion that Melbourne effectively became a source of soccer missionaries as economic migrants started to 'introduce' the game as they settled into Western Australia. In 1896 the Perth *Daily News* reported a flurry of growth across the football codes. In 'the British Association, the clubs already formed are the Perth, Crusaders, and Civil

Service, while a recently arrived Victorian, Mr. Stanton, is now engaged organising another team'.[197]

Soccer historian Philip Mosely argues that during the 1890s 'many coalminers from the eastern states flocked west with the onset of the Depression. They sought work on the Goldfields and in the process established soccer clubs at Kalgoorlie, Coolgardie and Boulder City'.[198]

In Western Australia soccer underwent a rapid growth in 1896 after the cooperative venture with Rugby Union that was inaugurated in 1892 failed to last beyond 1893. In a typical process of re-formation, a letter appeared in the press calling on Association footballers to form a club and players responded in numbers. Perth soccer historian, Richard Kreider cites a letter by 'An Old Reptonian' on 6 May that kicked-off the discussion.[199] It received an immediate response:

> I perused with pleasure 'An Old Reptonian's' letter
> published in your issue of today, in which he expresses the
> desirability of forming an English Association Football
> Club. As one of the committee of the now defunct club,
> to which 'An Old Reptonian' refers, I would inform him
> that it was solely the want of a suitable playing ground
> that rendered it impossible to continue the Association
> game. There was no lack of enthusiasm on the part of
> the members, and very little difficulty was experienced
> in arranging matches. I would suggest, therefore, that a
> meeting of all those interested in the English Association
> game be called at once to discuss the idea of forming a new
> club, when the question of securing the use of a ground
> might also be considered.[200]

Levels of enthusiasm suggested by the correspondent raise the question of activity in the absence of organised soccer between 1893 and 1896. It is probable that they kept playing at an informal level on the less-than-adequate grounds, especially given the game's near instant recovery upon reorganisation.

As Kreider points out, a 'spate of spirited replies' through the same newspaper, together with a clear backing from some of Perth's influential administrators, saw organised soccer get underway on Saturday 30

May 1896'.[201] The game took hold in Perth, initially with a four-team competition, and then spread to the goldfields and the Perth hinterland, with a substantial soccer presence established in Kalgoorlie, Southern Cross and Albany by the turn of the century.

Yet by the early 1900s football writing across the codes came to be couched in the terms of struggle and war, and although the Western Australian press housed a number of soccer-friendly writers, it also provided a platform for some particularly antagonistic perspectives. Tropes of invasion, patriotism and the brainwashing of children emerged, amplifying the lower-key dismissal of soccer as an anodyne force in Victoria. In something of a twist, soccer's entry from the east into Western Australia engendered resentment and hostility from an earlier eastern wave, the now entrenched Australian Rules proponents in the west.

'The British Association game is not, it must be said, a favorite with the Fremantle public,' reported the *Daily News* in Perth in June 1900.

> The latter are, perhaps, somewhat conservative (or patriotic) in their inclinations, and they look upon the alleged 'true football' as a foreign matter, with which they have no sympathy. The Australian game was built up of the best features of Rugby and British Association football, and the average Australian, or such of him as live in Victoria, South Australia, and Western Australia, is content with it. He can see no merit in Rugby or the British Association play, and no amount of exhibition of either game will induce him to alter his views in this matter.[202]

The article went on to argue, perhaps with some justification, that while soccer may be a good game when played at its best, it was not as well played in Western Australia. A year later the *Inquirer & Commercial News* raised the stakes. 'Follower' observed that Australian Rules 'is fully alive to the fact that an insidious attempt is being made to instil a love for the British Association game into the hearts of the schoolboys in this colony':

> Personally, I don't think those who are so striving will achieve their object, but it is well for the lovers of the Australian game to endeavor to checkmate the move in its

incipient stage. This is not a place for arguing the relative
merits of the two games. But the Australian game is the
national one – the very name proves that – and it is the
one that should be taught the schoolboys of Australia. It
is almost wholly played in Victoria, South Australia, and
Tasmania – the vast majority play it here, and it is gaining
ground in New South Wales and Queensland. Let the
lovers of the British Association play the game they were
taught in the old country, but not interfere with the boys
born in Australia, whose natural leaning is to play the
Australian game.[203]

No longer is the soccer commentary merely about unpopularity,
peculiarity and foppish British-degeneracy; tropes of cultural struggle,
propaganda, resistance, insidious brainwashing and interference with
children have entered the discourse. The tautological and absurd argument
that effectively runs: 'We've dubbed the game Australian Football: which
proves that it's the national game: which means that schoolboys should
play Australian Rules', inadvertently exposes the exclusory nationalistic
politics of the very act of such a naming.

Not all of those involved saw the issues in such confrontational terms.
On the occasion of a combined Perth and Fremantle trip to Albany in
1901 a typical celebratory dinner was held in the evening after a game.
During the toasts:

> Mr Collier proposed the toast of the 'British Football
> Association of Western Australia', coupled with the name
> of Captain White. He referred to the growing popularity
> of the game, and mentioned that there were in the colony
> at the present time, 24 senior, 12 junior and four school
> teams playing it. He touched on the great support given by
> Captain White to the game, and regretted the absence of
> Mr Alex. Peters, the general secretary of the Association.

> Captain White responded in happy terms. He said it was
> peculiar that the ex-chairman of the Association should
> propose the toast and he, the present chairman, should
> respond. He also spoke of the manner in which the British

game was growing in popularity and quoted figures to show the progress made daring the past few years. When the game was first taken up they battled for four seasons with senior teams only and they then recognised that they must also encourage juniors so as to provide material to recruit from. This had been done and last Christmas they had five school teams, and of the boys that left they formed four junior teams. The speaker also touched on an attempt that had been made to induce teams to come from England in the interests of instruction. The scheme, however, had not been taken up in the old country, but he hoped in the near future to have the assistance of two English coaches. Captain White spoke in flattering terms of Mr Collier and was confident that with his assistance the round ball in Albany would become more in evidence.

The Chairman proposed 'The visiting team' coupled with the name of Mr Lukyn. He said with many others in Albany he had seen British Association played for the first time that afternoon. He must confess to being prejudiced in favor of the Australian game, but he could understand why British Association men never took to any other game. He thought the British game was certain to increase in popular favor.[204]

Soccer's rhetoric was of trying to grow and find places where it could spread its influence, a strategy guaranteed to promote disquiet when a dominant code feels insecure in its standing. The old chestnut of the would-be beneficial English tour was also raised. The chairman's response to the speeches was warmly welcoming and yet appropriately assertive of his own game's value.

The article also mentions the strategy of negotiating a presence in the schools, a development that surpassed anything that had occurred in Melbourne, where the point of the Association seemed to be more about the players than the game. The strategy began in 1900 with four teams, a number that trebled in two years. By 1902 'Referee' in the West Australian was able to record a 'satisfactory increase of entries' in the schools' competition. Twelve teams had nominated for the coming season: Cottesloe, Claremont, Subiaco, Leederville, Newcastle-street, Highgate Hill, Perth Boys, East Perth, Midland Junction and three teams from Fremantle.[205] For the next decade or so, soccer seemed to be the preferred game within many Perth schools.

The 'soccer in schools' strategy and the Australian Rules response indicated a growing tension between codes and a struggle that both sides considered vital in the development of their games in Perth and beyond. Local Australian Rules authorities were determined to resist the soccer push into schools; soccer authorities were keen to stay there and expand.[206] In 1905 an Australian Rules writer from the *Daily News* framed the issue as an ongoing battle between *Australian* footballers and *English* teachers, lamenting that the State School Athletic Association had decided 'not to be bothered … with the Australian game in the schools' and accusing it of foisting soccer 'upon an unsuspecting, and unwilling public'.[207]

The writer subsequently mentions the formation of the 'Young Australian League' (originally the Young Australian Football League), an Australian Rules organisation whose name has clear nationalistic overtones.

Historian Richard Cashman dates the formation of the YAL at around the same time, over the same issue. He cites Victor Courtney's biography of the League's founder, John (J J) Simons, which explains the motive, while Cashman himself points out the contradiction:

> A deputation to the State Education authorities in 1905 was informed by a 'pompous official' that 'the Australian game was not to be played by schoolboys and that was the end of it'. Promoting Australian football against this perceived threat was a core activity of the League even though Simons conveniently ignored the fact that Australia's indigenous football game had descended from British football in the 1850s.[208]

This tendency to aggressive nationalistic rhetoric was to be expected in a period in which Australian Rules' peak body, the Australasian Football Council (AFC) and the VFL asserted as a matter of policy the game's 'national' origins and its primacy as Australia's football code. The language of war, struggle and patriotism came to dominate in a new phase of activism in Australian Rules in which the 'home' and 'colonised' states needed to be defended from invasion and counter-invasion, and the 'rugby states' needed to be colonised and converted. This desire found its ultimate expression in the modified Federation slogan, 'One Flag, One Destiny, One Football Game', adopted by the AFC in 1908.[209]

In Perth the *Daily News* reported on the formation of the AFC in November 1905 as 'an important event in the history of the Australian game':

> Up to the present, though the guidance of the Victorian League has generally been followed in some points, the other States have interpreted the laws in their own way. The conference was called with a view to overhauling the laws and making them more definite, and also to see what could be done in the way of further promoting the interests of the game throughout the Commonwealth and New Zealand. With this in view, an Australasian Council was decided upon to consider all aspects of the game, and to make recommendations to the various States' associations. The council is to be comprised of two delegates from each State, the Sydney League to have one and the Broken Hill Association one delegate each; the Goldfields and the Coastal Association in Western Australia will have one delegate each; North and South Tasmanian Associations will be represented by one delegate each, and the North and South Islands of New Zealand by one delegate each. The secretary of the Victorian League is to be the secretary and convener of the council, which will hold its first meeting in Melbourne in November, 1906. Thereafter it is supposed that the council will hold triennial meetings. The seventeen gentlemen comprising the conference from all the States and New Zealand set about their work most earnestly.[210]

It was an understandable rationalising process for a game that had not quite established common aims, goals and rules around Australia. The report then moved into a more ideological mode, recognising that 'the game was purely Australian in its characteristics, and in keeping with the federal spirit, the desire to make it the leading winter game, for all Australia was very strong'.

In keeping with this belief, the AFC adopted a propagandist attitude:

> It was decided that each association should set aside a certain percentage of its funds for what was termed 'propaganda work,' that is, of making converts among schoolboys. In Sydney, Queensland, and New Zealand Rugby has a strong hold, and in Western Australia both Rugby and British Association football are played, the latter game being fostered by English school masters in the public schools.[211]

In 1906 the AFC formally moved to align this propaganda work with the VFL's ' "propaganda fund", as they themselves called it, which was used for the advancement of the game in Victoria and elsewhere'.[212] The AFC moved that it 'should be topped up by a contribution of 5 per cent of all net gate receipts … in order to counter some of the gains that were being made by other codes in other areas'.[213]

The Adelaide *Advertiser* reported on the discussion of the 'propaganda fund' at the AFC meeting in Melbourne on 27 August 1908 during which the delegates complained about the pressures they were feeling from other codes:

> Messrs. Butler and Nash (NSW) pointed out that their league had to fight a formidable competitor in the Rugby Association, which had outbid them for the leading playing grounds. The New Zealand and Queensland delegates said they were faced by a similar difficulty.[214]

The WA delegate, J Webb, complained once more of soccer in schools. 'The difficulty of his league,' he said, 'was to compete with the English schoolmasters in the public schools of his State, who encouraged their pupils to play the British Association game.'[215]

Perhaps this complaint fell on partially deaf ears, because while the Council 'resolved to continue the 5 per cent levy but to exclude Western Australia and Tasmania from participating in the fund', it also resolved to disburse the funds to the 'Rugby states': '50 per cent to New South Wales, 30 per cent to Queensland, and 20 per cent to New Zealand'.[216] Perhaps the practical issue of grounds was deemed to be more urgent than the ideological issue of the influence of teachers on soccer. The decision may also represent the Council's confidence of their game's enduring appeal in the 'established' states.

Soccer in schools also became an issue in South Australia. The following piece is from the Broken Hill *Barrier Miner* in 1912:

> The arrival of so many immigrants has got the English styles of football going great guns in cities where the Australian game was practically the only one played. Still followers of the locally made rules are not disturbed at the mild boom amongst the other fellows, pointing out that there is room for all. Still it must be a bit disquieting to them, to learn that the admirers of soccer were endeavoring to get their game introduced into the public schools, on the ground that there is less risk of accident in it than in any other style of football. If this attempt meets with the approval of the Education Department, I am prepared to see the South Australian League raise a noise loud enough to be heard all over the Wheat State, and we may expect to see the South Australian Parliament prevailed upon to protect the home industry. It is at the schools that the footballers learn the rudiments of the Australian game. Therefore be prepared to hear the cry of 'Australia for the Australians' shouted aloud from the housetops if an attempt is made to make soccer the national brand of football.[217]

It begins with the language of tolerance and 'room for all' but soon enough shifts to the rhetoric of militant protectionism if the prime position of Australian Rules should ever be threatened.

Hess, Nicholson, Stewart and de Moore provide the context for understanding this new language of conflict as stemming from the 'propaganda' aims of the AFC/VFL. Yet they do so without acknowledging the place of soccer in the discord, leaving the tension as a bipolar one between Australian Rules and the Rugby codes, divided very much on Barassi-line principles.[218] The absence of soccer in Victoria in the period when the policy is being formulated certainly contributes to this perception of bipolarity, though the sheer energy of the dispute in Western Australia might have drawn more attention.

Even in Western Australia some correspondents sought to downplay the 'soccer threat', sometimes humorously. This response from 'Free Kick' in 1906 willfully forgets the vitriol of the previous five years:

> The British Association football authorities might well,
> after reading last Saturday's notes by 'Penalty' cry 'Save
> us from our friends!' 'Free Kick' has closely followed
> the football comments in the metropolitan Press during
> the present season, and, never once has he seen a hostile
> reference to the British Association game, the chief form of
> professional football in England.[219]

Even as he declared his innocence in the third person, 'Free Kick' nonetheless wielded the 'foreign game' epithet in full knowledge of the inferences that would be drawn and the mythologising work it would perform.

This vitriol continued to border on the absurd right up until the First World War. Inter-codal conversations in the Perth press were reduced to an unproductive, seemingly interminable tit-for-tat of whinge and counter-whinge. In 1908, a correspondent known as 'Penalty' wrote an exasperated defence of soccer to the *West Australian*:

> When one thinks of the handicap of junior soccer football
> in the way of suitable and accessible playing grounds and
> the awkwardness of the hour at which it mostly has to get
> going, one cannot help admiring the spirit that actuates the
> lads for a game which is unfairly stigmatised as 'imported'
> and un-Australian. These lads have not only to suffer
> sufficient handicaps in this way, but it is they who bear
> the brunt of unsportsmanlike criticism from companions
> who incline to another game . . . I feel it a duty to speak
> well of the Junior British Association for the fight they

are making for freedom of sport, and the right to pursue their recreation in whatever channel they think they can find most enjoyment. When these lads are met with such cries as 'dirty soccer,' 'imported game,' 'child's game,' and all the rest of the derogatory terms, they can always console themselves with the thought that Australians have nothing to say adversely to English cricket, which they play to perfection, and to the admiration of the sporting world, and which is none the less a clean and honest game, because it was 'imported.'[220]

'Penalty' drew a new element into the tension, one first intimated in reference to the collapse of soccer in 1893. The access to playing fields was an issue that was to intensify all around Australia as soccer grew rapidly prior to the First World War.

A 1912 report of a West Australian Football League (WAFL) meeting noted that a letter from the Modern School requesting permission to use the Subiaco Oval for soccer was met with derision. In the minutes of the meeting a delegate was quoted as saying: 'Oh! let's write and tell them that we will fix up all their grounds and fixtures for them! (Laughter)'.[221] The WAFL refused the request.

It is truly remarkable that dialogue like this found its way into minutes and then into the press. And while it seems an impractical and vain request it nonetheless foreshadows a spirit of vindictiveness, spite and nasty politics that guides the process of ground allocations for decades to come.

Another remarkable moment occurred in 1914 when a writer called 'Boundary' wrote in the *West Australian* about the issue of foul play in Australian Rules. He claimed that those 'at the helm do a lot, but they cannot accomplish every thing. Therefore they desire the co-operation of all well-wishers in tabooing the foul player, and anything that would tend to hinder the progress of soccer'.[222]

Bizarrely, in this construction, the integrity of Australian Rules is seen as secondary to the greater purpose of hindering soccer's progress. The syntax of expression makes it clear that at least some Australian Rules journalists had so internalised the rhetoric of the code war and its attendant soccerphobia that the battle against soccer is presented as the primary goal of Australian Rules supporters and journalists alike.

Soccer opponents were beginning to appear organised. For the first time we start to see football prejudice as more than simply the bias or taste of a journalist or correspondent, or the product of ignorance. It became what Welsh cultural theorist Raymond Williams called a 'structure of feeling', a structured attitude of preference, taste and discrimination generalised across a community.[223] Journalists and editors conveyed a particular sporting opinion in much the same way as they would be expected to hold a particular kind of political opinion, depending upon the newspaper's policy. The only difference was that in much sports' coverage in the southern and western states there seemed only one policy. While soccer had its press advocates in pre-war Perth, the renascent hegemony of Australian Rules was moving steadily into place.

## MELBOURNE REFORMATION

By the time soccer had reformed in Melbourne in 1908 the Australian sports context had changed. An age of relative innocence was over and a new competitive professional sports environment had emerged from the mists of amateurism. The nasty battles in Perth added three more invocations to the litany of soccer rejection: firstly, its brainwashing of children; secondly, its desire for grounds; and thirdly, its representing a counter-patriotic activity. A layer of ideological and political objections was added to the previously athletic, aesthetic or taste-based judgements. The promotion of Australian Rules in Melbourne and beyond shifted from being a simple cultural preference to an act of political duty, a duty that some journalists started to take seriously. Even in the bastions of amateurism prejudice was strong. In 1910 the *Barrier Miner* reported that the Melbourne 'University Sports Union debated the question of extending the University "blue" to Rugby football, but the players of the Australian game opposed vigorously the encouragement of what they called a foreign game, and the proposal was defeated'.[224]

The casual bias of the Melbourne press had been obvious for many years, but this notion of a more systemic bias was also becoming clear to some. C T Thomas, the manager of the WA soccer team touring the eastern states, had learned from experience in 1909 that in 'Melbourne a good deal of prejudice existed against the game, even among the press, but many leading men had been sympathetic towards it'.[225] The prejudice Thomas observed lies in the failure to acknowledge that which might otherwise seem to be newsworthy.

'The public might have been curious but the local media seemed loath to look into the tourists' intentions,' wrote Kreider. 'In South Australia, all the city newspapers interviewed Thomas and gave the team a respectable amount of print space. But in Melbourne, it was entirely different story – save for a scant report in an evening tabloid.'[226]

Thomas was, however, positive in his assessment of the attitudes encountered everywhere else:

> Their receptions in the other States had been marked by
> a friendly spirit, and there was no doubt that 'soccer' was
> a 'federalising' game. It appealed greatly to the young
> Australians, and several members of his team were Western
> Australian born, and nearly half of them had learnt the
> game in Australia.[227]

The changed mood and the impending condemnation notwithstanding, soccer got off to a smooth if quietly received Melbourne renewal. The foregoing generalities are not borne out in journalistic practice in this period, except insofar as the game's coverage is lightweight. The soccer sins of the Melbourne press at this stage tend to be ones of omission and not commission.

Harry Dockerty is considered by many as perhaps *the* vital re-founding figure in the history of soccer in Victoria. Dockerty was a trained tailor and cutter who had left Scotland in his early twenties, arriving in Melbourne in 1907. He set up a successful business in Melbourne catering to the clothing needs of many local doctors.[228]

A passionate player and administrator with access to money and some influence, he was a central motivating force for the game. The Dockerty Cup, which he donated and presented to the victorious Carlton Club (ironically as St Kilda's losing captain in the final) in 1909, remains the premier cup tournament in Victoria.

On 21 July 1908 Dockerty inserted a note in the *Argus* asking those interested in forming 'a British Association Football League in Melbourne' to send their names to him at '259 Collins street'.[229] They and he acted promptly. On 25 July a further note read: 'British Association football players meet at Middle-park Hotel for the opening practice match at 3 o'clock this afternoon'.[230] Quite a number turned up and they got into the swing of things quickly. Only two weeks later the *Argus* made the following report:

> Members of the newly formed league met at Middle-park on Saturday, and played four practice matches, the principal one being between two select elevens. This match was so evenly contested, and the players so keen, that the large crowd must have thought it was a cup final. Most of the players have regained form, and several were conspicuous for their clever work. This is very gratifying to the executive committee, who are busy in arranging matches with visiting clubs, and they hope at an early date to entertain an interstate team. The committee have a big task in regard to the formation of clubs, and the sooner this is done the better, so that by next season league matches can be started without any delay.[231]

On 15 August the Association defeated a team from the SS *Persic* 6–1. And while the report suggests that the *Persic* players were tiring after a long sea voyage and let in four late goals, the result does indicate that the Melbourne players had their strengths.[232]

On 12 September the *Argus* reported that further practice matches were to be held at Middle Park:

> A large meeting of the British Football Association was held at the Orient Hotel last evening, at which several important matters were settled. By-laws, &c., were compiled, and eight district clubs formed so that a proper commencement will be made next season. Three practice matches will be held at Middle-park this afternoon, the principal one being between English and Scottish players, and as these teams are even a good match is expected. Players and members are requested to meet at the Middle-park Hotel (opposite Middle-park station) at half-past 2 sharp.[233]

The St Kilda British Football Club, 1909. Harry Dockerty is in the back row, third from the left. This photograph is described by the Museum Victoria as representing 'the start of soccer in Australia'. Once more an archival error obliterates the older histories of Australian soccer.

Courtesy of Museum Victoria.

It seems reasonable to assume that Dockerty had noticed a strong though latent demand for the game, particularly at the level of participation. He acted on that demand and in a few months a bustling and energetic culture had established itself at Middle Park in South Melbourne. The resumption of migration no doubt bolstered Dockerty's confidence and things seemed well in hand for the launch of a bumper season in 1909.

Before the season was out, however, another moment of cooperation occurred that confounds some of the truisms of the history of football in Melbourne. A game of soccer was played as a curtain raiser to the Victorian Junior (Australian Rules] Association final. It is a rare example of cooperation between Australian Rules and soccer. The *Argus* advertised the trial in its pages.[234]

As soccer quietly grew in Melbourne, the press and the VFL seemed not to take it as a serious threat. It seemed worth neither talking up nor talking down. The *Argus*'s 'Observer' wrote in July 1910:

Although the British Association game is being played
now by a good many clubs in Melbourne, and it is the
particular game which excites the wildest enthusiasm in
England, the same difficulties that hamper the Australian
game in Sydney, and the Rugby game in Melbourne, will
prevent its becoming really popular. At the same time,
there are always in the community enough Englishmen
trained to that particular game to constitute a few sides,
and keep it going. In their special spheres, each game can
afford to treat the others as in the hospitable and courteous
light of guests, but anything like serious rivalry does not to
my mind, come into the question. [235]

Two months later, the *Argus* claimed that though 'British Association
football was gaining popularity, it was not clashing with other sport,
because those who played it would not spend their time on any other
kind of football'.[236] While it was seen to have no claims on Australian
Rules footballers or spectators, and while grounds were not an issue for
dispute, soccer carried on unmolested.

Despite a flourishing eight-club and two-division competition the
*Argus* failed to take the game seriously on a regular basis until 1913. In
1912 the reports were sporadic and even Victoria's mauling of Tasmania
on the hallowed turf at the MCG failed to generate a great deal of
column space.[237] The game fared little better in the first part of 1913.
Match reports were sparse and usually minimal even though the papers
sometimes acknowledged a substantial interest.

Standing out from this meagre trend was an example of what today
might be called a 'feature article'. In July 1913 a long piece was published
expressing surprise and wonder at this game being played in Melbourne's
midst:

'Soccer,' the more popular of the British games of football,
has established a fair footing in Australia in the last few
seasons, though, like every other exotic, it must have a
hard battle to hold its own in public esteem with a purely
local and long-established game, to the points of which
Australians are bred from infancy. With the steady inflow

of people there is increasing room for an old-world game, and some twenty teams are now playing under British Association rules in or about Melbourne, considerably hampered, of course, by the fact that there are few, if any, enclosed grounds with level turf at their disposal. The annual match between teams representing England and Scotland, played on the Fitzroy ground on Saturday, had about 4,000 enthusiasts watching. It was an excellent opportunity for realising the merits of the game.[238]

While it referenced the peculiar, the unestablished and the exotic, it nonetheless reined in some of the other conventional prejudicial tropes. It allowed the game some quality and popularity and supportively bemoaned its lack of an enclosed ground.

And this was meant in good faith, because the author followed up with a comparative analysis that pointed out soccer's qualities rather than put it in a poor light against Australian Rules. Indeed, Australian Rules might be able to learn something from the game with some study. Instead of chuckling quietly about heading, the author celebrated it as an impressive skill:

The wonderful thing is to see men jump into the air, receive a round ball, heavier than ours on the crown of the head, and direct it just where they want it to go; the other point that impresses one is the remarkable accuracy with which the players kick the ball in all sorts of positions that would be impossible and disastrous to Australians. They meet it is it flies feet high in the air and drive it a long distance considering the shape and weight of the ball; but, of course, there is no drop kicking, and only in the case of the goalkeepers an occasional punt. The beauty of the game is its combination. Wanting what we call 'system' it would be nothing, and the longer you watch it the more you appreciate that point. Men are always playing for position, rarely if ever 'bullocking' it. The best of our men might learn a lot – develop entirely new and desirable points in the Australian game, by seeing a few matches at 'Soccer'.[239]

This article seemed to signal a change in mood, inaugurating a tendency to publish substantial match reports, culminating in the Dockerty Cup final report in October, which began: 'The match at Middle Park on Saturday between Yarraville and St. Kilda attracted a large crowd of spectators, who were treated to a fine exhibition of football'.[240] It captured some of the game's excitement and tension, describing Yarraville's 4–3 win at the death as a lucky one.

Immediately before the war the *Emerald Hill Record*, which published in and to the South Melbourne region in which much of the state's soccer occurred, sometimes surpassed the *Argus*'s growing coverage with relatively substantial articles on games in Albert Park.[241]

In June another long piece in the *Argus* seemed to amplify all of the positives of the previous year's feature article.[242] It spoke to the popularity and growth of soccer in Melbourne at this time, acknowledging crowds of sometimes between 2000 and 4000 in attendance at Albert Park. By comparison the weekend after this piece was published merely 3568 spectators turned up at the MCG to see Geelong beat Melbourne in the VFL, though this figure does seem to represent a lower crowd than was usual.

It is written by an outsider, one brought up on Australian Rules but who is sympathetic to soccer. He sees it as a migrants' game, even though locals are starting to get involved. Victoria's strength in a recent inter-colonial game against New South Wales was very much determined by its being made up of experienced migrant Scottish and English players as against the callowness of the native-born from the north. Soccer is seen to be technically skillful, a 'pretty' and 'clever' game, lacking the corruption of professionalism that has poisoned the 'Australian game'. Moreover, it has a referee who tends not to interfere and is respected.

This latter point leads to the fascinating implied claim that Australian Rules is a hotbed of corruption and match fixing:

'SOCCER' FOOTBALL.

GROWING POPULARITY.

A PLAYERS' GAME.

Organised by a few enthusiasts from England, who found the Australian game, even as it was played several years ago, not at all to their liking, British Association football now draws from 2,000 to 4,000 people to Middle Park every Saturday. That the internal growth of the Victoria Amateur Football Association now affiliated with the governing body in England, has been equally steady is shown by the fact that there are 22 clubs in Victoria, with a roll of about 500 playing members, while New South Wales has 130 clubs. Most of those who are satisfied to stand in the open all the afternoon, threatened by batteries of artillery and stray horses, were keen followers of the game before they reached Australia, but there is a growing percentage of local 'barrackers' who come down as curious sceptics, and soon find themselves fascinated by what is one of the prettiest and cleverest games in the world to watch. A game that will attract 100,000 Englishmen must necessarily have some good features, and these are beginning to be more and more recognised by many who are disgusted at the present condition of the Australian game. It might be thought that some of the supporters are won by the prospect of a free show, but no suggestion of that can be found in the appearance of the men and women round the side lines. To a great extent it is a family outing, and renewal of home ties.

Men who have seen the game at its best laugh when asked how the standard of play here compares with that in England, but the things that are done with the ball at Middle Park are eye-openers to followers of League football. The principles underlying British Association are the prevention of handling of the ball and the reduction of rules, and consequently interference by the umpire or referee, to minimum. The playing area is smaller than ours, and there are only eleven men a side, who stand all in their own half of the ground at the kick-off and play largely in their places, the attack being made by the five forwards– centre and inside and outside left and right. The goalkeeper is the only player allowed to handle the ball, and he may not run with it. This formation and the use of a spherical ball make the game clean and open. Passing becomes a feature of the play, and even the mediocre player seems able to direct the ball to any angle with any part of the foot, toe, or heel while running. Naturally, the round ball is easier than the oval to deal with but the precision with which it is got under control from the air and 'dribbled' along a few inches in front of the feet at top speed is only less surprising than the use made of the opposite end of the body. Meeting the ball on the full a player will 'head' it across to the wing with the front of his skull farther than an Australian would pass with his hand. A man prominently connected with a sport once as popular as football, but killed by corruption, was keenly interested in the play on Saturday, and speculated as to the result if first-class League players acquired the same control over the ball as these amateurs. As he spoke an incident capped his remark. The ball flew high to the wing. A man 'headed' it back. An opponent headed it out again and a fellow of the first smothered it with his foot as it landed, and swung it hard towards the goal.

After the skill of the players the insignificance of the referee's part is the most striking feature. Imagine a league umpire in boots and blazer, walking about the centre of the ground most of the time! The only penalties he has to inflict are for handling the ball or the man, charging in the back, tripping and kicking, and 'offside.' But when he speaks he speaks with authority. Any player can be ordered off the ground. An incident on Saturday showed the spirit of the game. A player was tripped and he turned and kicked his opponent. Shouts of 'Play the game' came from both teams and as the referee merely warned the kicker and gave a penalty against him, a burly spectator growled. 'And he didn't order him off. No wonder the game doesn't get on in the colonies'.

Still, it does get on and its supporters even prophesy that it will solve the problem of universal football. Australians are not yet excelling as players, for their speed is counteracted by a lack of restraint. That is why Victoria won all four matches against New South Wales recently.

One has only to listen to the shouts of the players and
the keenest supporters to discover where they hail from.
But they hold that the morals of the game will win a way
for it. Already the round ball has made its appearance
in school playgrounds. The prime advantage claimed
for British Association is that to achieve corruption one
must buy most of the team. The referee has so little to
do in comparison with the Australian umpire that he is a
valueless asset.[243]

This article is possibly one of the first 'sleeping giant' articles published
in Melbourne. Rarely, if ever, before has the game been described in such
glowing terms by a Melbourne journalist. Not only is it optimistic, it
gives a solid foundation for such optimism. And it represented a massive
change from the muffled silence of years gone by. The *Argus* breathlessly
followed the four scoreless hours of the 1914 Dockerty Cup final and its
replay between Thistle and Northumberland and Durhams without so
much as a peep of complaint that no goals were registered.

Soccer was again on the edge. But this time it was on the edge of
entering the mainstream of sport coverage in Victoria. While it had
grown rapidly in Melbourne, other cities around Australia experienced
similar levels of interest and participation. In every major city there was a
soccer competition forcing itself into the consciousness of the population
via a media that was either doing its job or was forced to acknowledge
the game through various forms of pressure.

Nothing could stop it now – at least nothing short of an Imperial war.

## HALTED IN ITS TRACKS

The First World War put a stop to soccer in Perth and Melbourne and most
other places in Australia. Overwhelming commitment to the Australian
Imperial Force (AIF) by soccer players meant that competitions in both
states lost almost all of their substantial momentum.

But the momenta were different. Soccer culture in Perth was rich, but it
was also embroiled in ongoing battles with Australian Rules. Strongholds
were established and beachheads were constantly being created and
destroyed in schools, regions and communities. These polarities were

captured within and between newspapers with contrary or antagonistic views sitting side-by-side in the sports pages. The rhetorics of dismissal and opposition, victimhood and bullying were never far from the surface in Perth football writing in the pre-war period.

Melbourne was a more sedate story. Australian Rules was by far the most dominant game in spectator terms – though one report has soccer's total senior playing numbers falling only just short of 600 players before the war.[244] The monolithic code dominated the newspapers while soccer obtained minor though consistent notice. Very little in the way of nasty and soccerphobic rhetoric can be found in Melbourne newspapers during the period, probably because the game is never figured as a threat to 'Australian culture' the way it was in Perth. While soccer seemed to creep up on and startle the press shortly before the war and even if some journalists (perhaps inspired by their Perth colleagues) *were* sharpening their pencils in preparation for some choice anti-soccer writing, the opportunity for soccer-bashing was rarely taken up by Melbourne journalists until well after the First World War.

# CHAPTER 5

# RURAL SOCCER BEFORE
# THE FIRST WORLD WAR

Immediately before the First World War soccer appeared as if it would come to inhabit the whole continent of Australia. The wave of migration from the British Isles had begun to settle across the country giving soccer an energetic critical mass that enabled it to rise across the nation.

'The news of the formation of clubs to play "Soccer" at Murwillumbah, Tweed River, and Broken Hill is very pleasant to supporters of the game,' reported the *Sydney Morning Herald* in March 1912. 'The Queensland Association is taking an active part in the movement on the Tweed, for clubs formed in that locality will, in view of the distance from headquarters in New South Wales, be allowed to affiliate with the Queensland body. A Queensland tour, taking in the Tweed, should soon become popular among New South Wales players, for branch associations are rapidly developing in Ipswich, Toowoomba, Mount Morgan, and Rockhampton.'

The *Herald* also reported 'great strides in the advance of the game in Tasmania' and that 'a scheme of inter-district matches' were to be held to determine a 'thoroughly representative team'.[245]

A series of selection games between representative teams were played in the eastern states. In New South Wales, Sydney, Granville and district, and South Coast provided teams. In Queensland teams from Brisbane, Toowoomba and Ipswich and West Moreton took part in the process. The Tasmanians held trials between the south and the newly formed northern association before selecting their team to tour Victoria and New South Wales.

Yet, for every advance in the game, negative voices lurked. In April 1911 the *Worker*, the often xenophobic and racist newspaper attached to the rural sector of the Australian labour movement, reported on a 'new' game being introduced in Queensland. Adopting a pose of *faux* ignorance, 'Half-back' wanted 'to know what British "Soccer" football is, which it is proposed to introduce into Queensland'. The *Worker* answered:

> The 'Soccer' game is that played under the rules of the
> British Football Association. It is, perhaps, the most popular
> of the winter outdoor games in the old country and is played
> to a certain extent in the capitals of the Australian States.
> Australians, however, don't appear to relish it, preferring
> either the Australian rules game or Rugby.[246]

The *Worker*'s distinction between city and rural Australians was illustrative. Soccer inhabits the capitals but 'Australians' do not relish the game. In the world view promulgated by the *Worker*, rural Australians were the *real* Australians and so, necessarily, soccer was not *real* Australia's cup of billy tea.

'Half-Back' might have consulted the newspaper's own archives and saved himself the trouble of asking the question. In 1898 the *Worker* had in fact reported positively on soccer's attempts to attach itself to the Queensland labour movement by participating in the May Day celebrations.[247]

Not only did the 1911 *Worker* rhetorically forget its own archival past reporting on the game, it also falsely declared a contemporary absence of soccer in rural Australia, despite the game's having been played in a number of Queensland rural centres many years prior to the article's publication. Soccer had a presence in small towns like Esk, Stanthorpe and Oakey and in major regional centres like Townsville, Rockhampton and Toowoomba. And had the *Worker* and its affiliate union, the Australian Workers' Union, been more *au fait* with mining culture it might have been forced to adopt a different tack when it came to assuming the absence of soccer outside of the major Australian cities. The Central Queensland mining town of Mount Morgan hosted soccer matches as early as 1894 and Charters Towers, the North Queensland mining town, had been a soccer stronghold since 1891. It was a popular sport in a town of 30,000 people at its peak.

In the coalmining regions, soccer was even more popular. In fact a soccer club or competition was established in just about every coalmining community in Australia at some point prior to the First World War.

'Next season,' wrote one Western Australian correspondent in 1900, 'I do not expect to hear of any mining camp mustering a dozen men where there is not at least one British Association club going.'[248]

Even in country Victoria coalmining towns in this period were likely to host a soccer team or competition. Labour historian Andrew Reeves writes of the effects of migration on the coalmining town of Wonthaggi in Eastern Victoria. 'Only on Australian coalfields, it seems, could soccer rival rugby or Australian Rules Football at that time. In Wonthaggi, too, it remained a sport with appeal to specific groups, as the name "Wonthaggi Thistles" and the "Caledonians" suggest'.[249] The nearby Gippsland mining communities of Mirboo North and Mirboo South also had soccer teams, possibly as early as 1910.[250]

In Queensland's agricultural centres, soccer received a strong boost from migration. The rapid growth of soccer in the Darling Downs is given context when the size of the migration is understood. In June 1911 over 600 migrant 'navvies' from Britain arrived in Moreton Bay and were dispersed in their cohort groupings to various centres around the region from Warwick to Dalby to Kingaroy to mining, railway-construction and farm-labouring jobs. The *Brisbane Courier* reported that 'the 220 workers sent to Oakey were practically all Scotsmen, and similarly men from Bristol, Birmingham, Manchester, Ireland, and other localities were, as far as possible, kept together'.[251] Even as these men sat in their boats in Moreton Bay awaiting a landing and facing the daunting prospect of settling in a new country, sport was not far from their thoughts. The *Courier* adjudged that from 'the remarks of the men it appears very likely that "soccer" football and other athletic combinations are to be formed, and where possible they will try conclusions with similar bodies in towns and districts near the works'.[252] It is highly likely that the 220 Scotsmen had some impact on soccer in Oakey, a town in which the game had been played since at least 1907.[253]

Despite the narrative pushed by the *Worker*, soccer inhabited a significant place in rural Australia by 1914. Its historiographical and mythological absence in the tales of the bush hides the fact that the game took its place. In regional centres across Australia there flowered sometimes fragile but always committed soccer competitions.

When examined in isolation, these bush soccer competitions look like tenuous enterprises, spluttering into action and readily stuttering into decline. Sometimes they restart only to collapse again after a brief rise. The isolated longitudinal analysis of soccer in any given rural centre is liable to create an impression of weakness and inevitable failure, encouraging the belief that when soccer makes an appearance it comes as a stranger in the camp, stays for a while and then leaves, usually to be forgotten and wiped from memory. When the development of soccer is seen in concert across towns and regions, however, the picture looks very different. Patterns of establishment and re-establishment across the twentieth century in towns like Broken Hill, Cairns, Darwin, Geraldton, Goulburn, Horsham, Mildura, Mount Isa, Murwillumbah, Northam, Petersburg, Queanbeyan and Warwick suggest something more solid, a nationwide movement bound to regather and re-emerge wherever and whenever it stumbles.

## SOCCER SPOTFIRES

In the immediate pre-war period 1912 seems to be the year of soccer's most rapid growth. If March saw widespread soccer preparations across the country, June heralded the beginning of something that could be described as a nationwide spate of soccer spotfires.

Firstly, on Saturday 1 June a notice appeared in the *Warwick Examiner and Weekly Times* advising that a local in the south-east Queensland town of Warwick, Mr W G Smith, had 'procured a British Association football, and all interested in this game will have an opportunity of having a game by meeting Mr Smith at Slade Park this afternoon'.[254]

Secondly, two days later the *Argus* reported an impressive result in what was probably the first-ever game for a Warrnambool team.[255] While Mr Smith and friends were gathering at Slade Park in Warwick, Queensland, Warrnambool were exceeding expectations against a second-division team from Melbourne: 'A British Association football match was played in the Friendly Societies' park on Saturday afternoon between the Wallabies, the [junior] metropolitan unbeaten team, and a Warrnambool team. The Warrnambool team won by 6 goals to 1'.[256]

Thirdly, a further two days later the *West Australian* reported that Northam (100 km east of Perth) could not emulate Warrnambool's feat when it played *its* first-ever game (also on 1 June), suffering what was described as a 'creditable' 5–2 loss to Fremantle's Second-Division team.[257]

Fourthly, ten days later in the far west the *Geraldton Guardian* noted: 'We understand that there is some possibility of a British Association Football Club being formed in Geraldton. Several enthusiasts were seen indulging in the game on Saturday, and it is stated that it is likely steps will be taken to form a club'.[258]

Yet the temptation remains to see these as isolated outbursts outbreaks of soccer, especially given the rhetoric of isolated marginality deployed in the Warwick and Geraldton reports. One man and several enthusiasts cut lonely figures, desperately seeking fellow soccer players with whom to have a kick. The distances involved in the Northam and Warrnambool games bespeak another kind of loneliness, that of the long-distance footballer. Sometimes even whole teams were figured as being alone. The year before, the *Northern Star* in Lismore had noted a similarly isolated soccer enterprise in Oakland (west of Coonabarabran, New South Wales):

> The Oakland club have withdrawn from the local [Rugby] competition. It is the intention of the members to play 'soccer' football, and for that purpose the ground is being got into readiness. Owing to a goodly number of immigrants who have a good knowledge of the game having obtained employment in the local mill, Oakland should be able to put a good team in the field, but the query is who are they going to play against?[259]

The team played at least once, winning well against Coraki in 1911, but there seems to be little other trace and their story soon vanishes from the record.

Rounding out June 1912's first 'footers', Goulburn hosted an exhibition game between two teams from the Granville district in Sydney – though the event was not without its typically soccerite organisational glitches as indicated by the report's headline, 'Forlorn Footballers':

> Two of our district teams, Holroyd and Merry Farmers, some 36 in all, went by invitation to Goulburn, to play an exhibition Association match on the holiday. Unfortunately, by some strange oversight, no arrangements

had been made for their reception or accommodation, and the unhappy Soccer players found themselves far from home, and with no place whereon to rest their weary heads. The hotels seemed to be all full; the police were applied to, and the kindly officials made the telephone wires red hot as they rung up the various publicans and boarding-house proprietors in their zealous efforts to obtain beds for the visitors. It was not until about 3am on Monday that sleeping accommodation was found, the Granville boys having in the meantime been wandering about the town, making the best of the trying circumstances, but not exactly fitting themselves to give a highly finished exposition of tip-top Soccer in a few hours' time. The match, however, came off, and was won by Merry Farmers, the score being 2 to nil. It was about 9 at night when the tired party returned to Granville and they were loud in their denunciations of the someone whose blunder had turned out so uncomfortably for them.[260]

More first instances were to follow. Cairns re-booted in early July after a two-year break: 'It was decided to try and run three teams this season, viz. Railway Rovers, Rangers, and Sawmills, and by the enthusiasm shown at the meeting there should be a great revival of the "Soccer" game in Cairns'.[261] And Queanbeyan's first game followed towards the end of the month: 'In the Soccer match, Department of Home Affairs v. Royal Military College, the former won by three goals to one. The proceeds of the gate will be handed to the local hospital and we understand the amount will be over £5'.[262] The *Rockhampton Morning Bulletin* notes that the first game of soccer in Emerald in Queensland was played on 25 August 1912.[263]

## WARWICK: A CASE STUDY

It is not known how many turned up to the inauspicious 1 June beginnings on Slade Park near the centre of Warwick. The turnout was probably not large. Nonetheless, enough enthusiasm was mustered for the *Warwick Examiner and Weekly Times* to be able to report four weeks later that a club had been formed and they were expecting a 'good roll up of players'.[264] And that seemed to be that; an association had been formed. Interest was sought from around the district and Warwick, Clifton and a team from the nearby coalmining town of Tannymorel began to play soccer against one another.

The earliest recovered press reference to actual play is to a match on 28 July in which Warwick easily defeated Clifton:

> A British Association 'soccer' game was played on the reserve, between a Warwick team (under Capt. Willis) and a local team (Capt. Graham). This was the first time this game was played in Clifton, and it attracted a good attendance, including many ladies. After a well-contested game, Warwick won by 11 to nil.[265]

The Warwick team faced a more difficult challenge against Tannymorel on 19 August. Not a game for the faint-hearted, it resulted in serious injuries for two of the combatants.[266]

By September the Warwick club had broadened its horizons to incorporate Toowoomba and, in the first recorded clash between the two towns, Warwick won 4–1. Toowoomba won the return clash a few days later 3–0. The Warwick Club rounded out the 1913 season with another game against Tannymorel on 28 September, which was a 1–1 draw.

Whence did these players emerge? Certainly migration and settlement, and the coalmining industry brought many of them to the region. But surely they did not all turn up in May 1912, itching for a game of 'footer' or 'fitba' or whatever they called it, and simply start playing? The 600 'navvies' of June 1911 may have had an impact on the region but the rapid escalation suggests a great deal of latent desire for soccer already inhabiting the district, a desire that was only given embodiment after Mr Smith's acquisition of a ball, his decision to invite all-comers to play and the implied promise of organisation. It cannot be known for how long that desire had been stirring. All that can be known is that it was there and seemingly raring to be tapped.

The next report was from the following season. The *Examiner* on 2 July 1913 indicated that two games had already been played by Warwick against Tannymorel, both losses. The writer expected that Warwick would be out to make amends on the coming Saturday.[267] The game-day *Examiner* noted that 'members of the Warwick team and officials will meet at Stephens' studio, in Grafton-street at 2.30, for the purpose of being photographed as a group'.[268] Maybe the dose of 'stardom' worked because the Warwick players turned the tables, winning 1–0.

No doubt it was getting repetitive playing the same opponents each time and so a game was arranged against the local Rugby team on 12 July:

> This afternoon in McLaughlin's paddock, at 3 o'clock,
> all players are requested to be in attendance when a team
> will be selected to take part in what will prove to be a
> somewhat unique fixture in Warwick football circles. A
> prominent Rugby team in Warwick has consented to meet
> the local soccer players at their own game next Saturday
> afternoon, and, as at least half the team understand the
> British Association rules, the match should be entertaining
> as well as interesting.[269]

The fact that half the team understood the rules is telling. It suggests that the game was not foreign to a good proportion of Warwick footballers. It also gives strength to the argument about latent soccer desire.

Challenges soon came thick and fast from other clubs and communities in the region:

> The Warwick Soccer team has been asked by the Walloon
> and Rosewood Soccer Football team to play them a match
> in Warwick on Thursday, 28th August. The Warwick team
> will endeavour to fulfil the fixture, but would prefer that
> the match should be played on a Saturday. In any case the
> visitors will have a match in Warwick.[270]

Throughout the season the Warwick team also organised fixtures against the 'Wanderers' and the Ipswich Railway Employees team. It rounded out this season with two games against Toowoomba. The first was a thrilling 4–4 draw, with Warwick losing the return match 3–0, a number of locals missing because of 'business exigencies'.[271]

The report on the 4–4 draw is a remarkable document. For a start it is an example of the absurdly long soccer report, especially when placed in comparison with any other *Examiner* soccer report from the period. It also constructed soccer as an important local event. Some other politics were not far below the surface. The reference to the reprehensible behaviour of the Rugby team also points to some local political shenanigans. But most intriguing, and important, of all is its suggestion that 'Toowoomba was generally regarded as the nursery in Queensland of British Association football'.[272] This status as a powerhouse is long forgotten.

In 1914 the competition resumed. Games were played against Allora and Tannymorel (one of which was a benefit for a Tannymorel player who had lost his sight in a mining accident) and, towards the end of the season, Yangan.

This series of reports invites the conclusion that the game as played in the Warwick region was burgeoning. Each month seemed to draw a new town or community into the local soccer fold. Not only were the numbers and participation impressive, Warwick was also competitive on the field. It had held its own against 'the nursery', the Toowoomba team that had supplied three players to the Queensland state team in 1912. The story had only just begun and was pregnant with massive potential.

As is the case with so many of the blossoming soccer competitions around rural Australia, driven by migrant workers and schoolteachers, the Great War stepped in to take away many of the young men who were playing the game. From the Toowoomba region alone, 140 soccer players went to the Front. In most parts of Australia, including the big cities, soccer became unviable. Warwick was no different. A few games involving Warwick were played at a junior or cadet level, but soccer was effectively shut down for the duration of the war.

## AFTER THE WAR

As is the pattern around most of rural Australia, soccer in Warwick waited for the next wave of migration to give it players to reinforce its returned men. The coal mines in the region inevitably brought more English and Scottish migrant soccer players to work them and the game lurched back into action in the mid-1920s, with Warwick playing in a healthy competition, with a recorded league table, against Allora, Mt

Colliery and Tannymorel for several years. The game waned in the early 1930s only to be revived once more in the middle of the decade (aided by a strong Stanthorpe influence).

The *Courier-Mail* reported on a particularly optimistic AGM of the Warwick Soccer Association in May 1936:

> At the annual meeting of the Warwick Soccer Association the president (Mr T Ingrams) expressed pleasure at the progress the code was making in Warwick, and the hope that it would not be long before Allora, Tannymorel, and Mt Colliery were again in the association. Warwick now possessed a ground second to none on the Downs.[273]

This is an enigmatic expression of optimism from a code about to head into a 30-year slumber in the region, yet it was a commonly held view in soccer communities around Australia at the time. They were not to know that another devastating war was on the horizon, one that would again drastically reduce the game's available players and create a new Australia in which soccer seemed less at home in many towns and regions than ever before.[274]

# CHAPTER 6

# BEHIND THE LINES

The photograph (overleaf) seems to represent an enigma: a team mostly of Victorian soldiers playing soccer and beating a team of English soldiers in France during the First World War must surely be a rarity. In truth, it is so common as to be banal. Sporting contests between Australian troops and their allies blossomed in all theatres of war for purposes of morale, fitness and recreation. Australian Rules, rugby and cricket were popular games. But there is an argument to be made that soccer was even more prevalent; first because it was far easier to find an opponent from within the British troops, second because soccer was a much more popular game in pre-War Australia than historians generally acknowledge, and third because soccer players tended to enlist with almost unanimous enthusiasm.

Today soccer is rarely remembered as a vital part of Australia's military history and the ANZAC legacy.[275] Yet the game contributed greatly in the First World War. In terms of moral support, enlistment, participation and 'sacrifice', soccer was at the forefront of sports-body commitment. While this commitment was sometimes remembered in the years immediately following the war, it did not take long to fade into memory.

## SPORT AND WAR

In contemporary Australia sport and war have obtained a close emotional connection. Relying on assertions of their cultural centrality and intimations of their contribution to war service, the two dominant football codes have assumed the right to put the sport–war connection front and centre. The AFL and the NRL each conducts intensely

'The photograph was forwarded from "Somewhere in France" by Corporal A. Shields. It is a team chosen from the 38th and 39th battalions, which played a game of "Soccer" behind the lines, against a combination of "Tommies." The Australians won by four goals to one. Reading from left to right the names are:-Back row – Pte. W. Martin (South Melbourne, 38th Batt.), Sgt. A. Geddes (Ballarat, 39th Batt), Cpl. A. Shields (Albert Park, 38th Batt.), Pte. G. Gregory (Bendigo, 39th Batt.), Pte H. King (Sydney, 38th Batt.). Middle row – Cpl. D.C. Honeyman (Lakemba, Sydney, 38th Batt.), Pte. F. Symons (Melbourne, 39th Batt.), Pte. H. Jansen (Melbourne, 38th Batt.), Pte H. Beasley (Richmond, 38th Batt.), Pte. D. Robertson (Castlemaine, 38th Batt.). Front row – Pte. H. Heaney (Melbourne, 39th Batt.), Pte T. Holmes (Prahran, 38th Batt.), Pte. H. Souter (Brunswick, 39th Batt.).'[276]
Courtesy of the *Weekly Times*.

publicised and popular ANZAC Day matches.[277] It is a tradition to which supporters of both codes have been drawn in large numbers and which coincides with the rejuvenation of the ANZAC legend in Australian cultural life over the past twenty years.[278]

Through this connection the dominant football codes have been able to insert themselves into mythologised narratives of the past and the present. One implied narrative is that Rugby League players from New South Wales and Queensland and Australian Rules players from the rest of Australia made up large sections of the fighting force, to the extent that in mythological terms the spirit of the soldiers and the footballers have crossed over and merged.[279]

Yet any present-day understanding that the two codes dominated military participation stems ironically from the very push designed to cover up professional Australian Rules and Rugby League players' tardiness in enlisting – the poorly subscribed Sportsmen's Battalions.[280] Sport historian Murray G. Phillips points out that several sports, 'like rugby league, boxing and Australian rules football, used the military units of sportsmen to rebut criticisms about continuing their activities during war time; other sports, which ceased their programmes, were involved because they considered it was their patriotic duty'.[281]

Some contemporary retellings of the role of football in war also help to cloud the issue. Dale Blair's 'Beyond the metaphor: Football and war, 1914–1918', published in 1996, conveys the sense that Australian Rules was the most significant sport played by Australian troops. Blair's article is based on the sound premise that 'Sport and war have long been synonymous with Australia's national identity and the ANZAC legend provides one of the great pillars upon which that identity has been built. Of equal, if not greater standing, is the nation's penchant for sport.' He also make the important observation that given 'the extent to which Australia's First World War experience permeates the national psyche, it is somewhat surprising that the implications of and influence of sport during this period have been largely neglected'.[282]

While Blair acknowledges 'the various football codes' and gestures towards the complex geneses of football in Australia, he makes a too-easy transition from the generalities of sport and football to the specificities of Australian Rules without properly negotiating the minefield of exclusion and forgetting that such a move involves. Sometimes he transitions from one generalised discussion of Australian Rules football to the next by citing specific evidence of a game or a practice that had no necessary connection with Australian Rules. For example, he discusses the practice of 'mobbing':

> The lack of proper playing fields, particularly of the large
> size required for Australian football, was always a problem.
> The 40th Battalion, a Western Australian unit, resolved
> the problem by devising their own game which they called
> 'mobbing'. It was played with a hessian bag filled with
> straw, and the game had no rules other than that the bag

could not be kicked. The basic object of the game was to force or throw the bag through the opposition's goal. The beauty of the game was that it could be played 'on any old ground'.[283]

Assumptions run deep in this passage. Blair seems not to countenance the possibility that the soldiers were not looking for a next-best activity to Australian Rules but were creating a game, from scratch, out of the equipment and conditions that were available to them. He possibly assumes that because they were a WA battalion they were Australian Rules footballers by default. Blair's elisions are symptomatic of a whole range of cultural practices through which hegemonic football codes assert and justify their contemporary dominance while rewriting the past in their own image.

## REPORTS FROM THE FRONT

Sporting contests were significant activities within the AIF during the First World War. Members of the armed forces gravitated to them in great number, whether as participants or spectators. Military authorities saw these contests as an important means of maintaining good morale and letting off steam, and the AIF went to great lengths to facilitate competition and even recognise sporting excellence with awards and trophies. Blair suggests that 'the Army patronised sport in many ways – including creating facilities and ovals and organising regimental teams and competitions – because sport enhanced fitness, boosted morale, provided a physical outlet and countered boredom'.[284]

There are a number of means through which this assertion can be sustained. Substantial official reports, and photographic and officer-diary records are housed at the Australian War Memorial.[285] These demonstrate a virtual Olympiad of sport across the theatres of war.

A significant indicator of sport's general role in the overseas AIF is contained not in detailed formal and informal accounts but in a simple brief list published broadly across Australia. Among many other newspapers, the *Camperdown Chronicle* contained a report in May 1916 claiming to have seen 'a cable from Cairo to headquarters.' The cable had urged: 'Send immediately six tents, 10 small pianos, 5,000,000 printed letter paper and envelopes, 50 sets of cricket material, 50 soccer footballs, 50 association footballs'.[286]

An under-utilised but particularly valuable source of information about how servicemen identified with this culture of military sport is contained in the many letters 'From the Front' published in the Australian press during the war.[287] A typical letter of this kind contained much discussion of sport, particularly football, played or observed by the author. Or it spoke glowingly of a footballer who had performed heroically and sometimes a strong correlation was constructed between prowess on the football field and in battle. The Adelaide *Register* noted that a number of letters:

> from soldiers at the front state that Pte. Stanley F. Carpenter has been recommended for the Victoria Cross. He is a native of Newcastle, and one of the best-known footballers in New South Wales. He has been playing football for 20 years, although only 36 years of age, and has represented New South Wales and Australia in interstate and international matches. He has always played with the East Newcastle Club and is a life member of the New South Wales Rugby League.[288]

Soldiers from the northern states often explicitly or implicitly identified as Rugby players or advocates. The following letter published in the *Warwick Examiner and Times* in February 1917 uses a group of Australian soldiers' familiarity with Rugby to explain their poor performance against an English soccer team:

> We all went down to a Tommies' camp recently and played a football match with them. They played 'soccer.' Of course Rugby is our game so the Tommies scored an easy win. We enjoyed ourselves very well looking on, as some very good players were on the field.[289]

The Barassi line is often drawn in the letters, with those from the northern states naturalising the rugby codes and those from the south and west naturalising Australian Rules. Some of the letters of soldiers from the Australian Rules states refer to the good-natured rivalry they have with advocates of the rugby codes.

Servicemen from the southern and western states sometimes expressed their frustration that games of Australian Rules were hard to come by in England. Similarly, they voiced a longing to see games at home. Private 'Jack' Brown wrote such a letter from Gallipoli on August 17, adding the rider that the footballers at home might be better placed in the armed forces:

> We get great instructions in case gas comes here, but so far they are playing the game. Good old North Launceston! Guess they will nearly be premiers this season, though it's time they gave up football and came along here. The more that come the sooner we will get home.[290]

The *Emerald Hill Record* was a vehicle for many such letters. Published in and to the South Melbourne district, it kept tabs on the South Melbourne Australian Rules footballers at the front. In 1917 it published a Roll of Honour for the club listing those players who had served and noting those who had been killed.[291] A number of these serving players wrote letters home 'from the front' and were published by the *Record*. South Melbourne's Wal Laidlaw was published around fifteen times in 1917 and 1918 and invariably mentioned football:

> A few more lines to let you know that I'm well. I am still receiving the [*Football Record*] regularly, which is most welcome. I was sorry to hear poor Bruce Sloss was killed. He was one of the best, but these things must be expected . . . Things were fairly quiet a week ago, so we had a football match between a couple of picked teams. We played in mud about six inches deep. One side played in sheepskin jackets and the other in shirts. After the first quarter it was hard to distinguish the difference between the players, as all were caked in mud. Our side won by seven points after the hardest day's toil I've ever done.[292]
>
> I will be looking forward to future papers for the results of the football. We are having a short rest, and we concluded our football season after playing eight matches, losing two.[293]

In the main the *Record's* focus is on Australian Rules football, though other codes and games get an occasional mention. Laidlaw wrote again: 'We have finished football, and were undefeated after playing twelve matches. Sport was booming through the winter, and our brigade had the champion Rugby and Australian team, besides the heavy weight boxing champion, so we did well'.[294]

The *Record's* function of keeping track of the South Melbourne players at the war is exemplified in the following letter from Private Frank Arnold, who had played for South Melbourne Football Club in the 1890s:

> I witnessed a football match between two battalions. It was a match well worth going to see. It was in the danger zone, but that did not make much difference. Tich Bailes was playing. He kicked four goals, but he is not the Tich of old. The —th had not been beat for two years. It was a terrible shock to them. One of our prominent officers took £30 to £90, and the rank and file all had their few francs on. I captained the —th Battalion. We won by a point just on time. This was when we were training on Salisbury Plains. Poddy Hiskins is not very far from where I am camped. I saw poor Bruce Sloss's grave. I would, very much like to send you a photo of it. I will do my best to do so. I have two of the old South footballers with me – Joe Lowrey and Bert Mills. Both wish to be remembered to you and all the old boys.[295]

A few months later Laidlaw regretted to say: 'I haven't come across any of the boys yet. At the present time it is difficult to get in touch with any of them. I suppose you will be thinking of the football season by the time this reaches you. I hope you have better luck this year. Kind regards to all'.[296]

Soccer obtains some direct mention in the letters. Private Marshall Caffyn was another ex-South Melbourne player, published a number of times in the *Record*. Here he reports on his own participation in a game of soccer:

> I had a game of footer the other Sunday – soccer. They put me in goals, and thought I was a marvel when kicking off – I used to put the old round ball half way up the ground

every time – the game is not much good. Give me the good
old Australian rules every time. I have also played rugby
over here. The games aren't to be compared.[297]

Les Turner, also a South Melbourne player, wrote from Scotland, 'I
went to see a British Association football match last Saturday. It was a
good display of their football and I enjoyed it, but give me our game
every time for top place'.[298]

This was an echo of a letter from Laidlaw, two years previously. He
had been 'to see an English soccer football match'. He thought the game
was 'interesting to watch', and that 'both teams were evenly matched.
They had some topnotch men, and the game was played at great speed'.
But, in the end he felt, 'there is nothing like our Australian game'.[299]

Soccer is acknowledged and enjoyed to an extent, but the letters display a
felt need to remind readers that it is an inferior, replacement activity for what
they would rather be doing. It is an interesting prefiguring of a significant
mode of the *Football Record*'s anti-soccer rhetoric in years to come.[300]

As VFL footballer Stan Hiskins writes, some bluntly refused to
participate: 'Every Sunday we have a game of soccer. We enjoy it too,
although most of our boys won't have it on any account'.[301] It is notable
that he is happy to try the game and enjoy it whereas some of his less-
accomplished comrades refuse.

Other sportsmen also took the opportunity to play soccer, while
expressing a yearning for their main sport at home, in the following case
cycling in Queensland. 'I am O.K. Still in the same old place, and not
likely to shift yet. I often get "Sports" and read up the cycling. I suppose
the racing season is starting again in Brisbane. The only sport we are able
to take up is football, and we had a good game of soccer today'.[302]

When soccer is discussed fully it is sometimes as a curiosity. The
following piece from Les Turner reports positively on a game he observes
but is written with a sense of the shock of the new:

I saw a great football match here the other day between
an Egyptian and a British army team. Football here is very
different to Australian. It is purely foot-ball – hands are not
allowed to touch the ball, which is perfectly round. I can see
it is a far more scientific game than ours, and the Egyptians

are particularly clever with their feet, and very active. The game is called soccer, and was introduced by the British 10 years ago. As it happened the British team won, but there was very little difference between the two teams.[303]

While Turner is complimentary towards the game he nonetheless sees soccer as exotic. His writing exemplifies the way that soccer has a curiosity status in many of the letters and, while it was often played by Australian troops, it is seen as a game to be played for second-hand reasons. It is what the locals played; it was the best available second-best to Australian Rules or a version of Rugby – and so could be enjoyed on that basis. Some letters also make it clear that when an opportunity to play their preferred code presented itself, soldiers took it with glee.

## SOCCER IS ORDINARY

If the evidence presented in many of these letters constructed soccer as a necessary yet tolerated second-hand indulgence, another stream of letters made a different point. They spoke to soccer's ordinariness in the military context.

Sometimes when Australian servicemen attended soccer matches they referenced a familiar 'home' code but came away with less certainty about the superiority of that code and felt less inclined to offer judgements. Private Edward J. Ryan wrote to his uncle in 1916: 'Well, I can tell you that football does not worry me much at present, but I went to look at a game of "soccer" while I was in Edinburgh, and I wouldn't like to pass my opinion as to which is the best game – Australian or "soccer".'[304]

One soldier's letter to the *Euroa Advertiser* alludes to home football colours (probably to Euroa Magpies Australian Rules FC) but fails to cast a judgement on what he had observed – apart from the inferred mild disappointment that his adopted team lost: 'Had a stroll through the glorious gardens and saw the teams from the H.M.S. *Swiftsure* playing soccer, and as one side appeared in black and white I got a bit excited. The red team won'.[305]

Many of the letters 'normalise' soccer without comparative reference to any other code. A soldier in Egypt in February 1915 describes soccer as explicitly un-exotic: 'They then started their football match. They played English soccer, so it wasn't anything novel'.[306] A letter from HMAS *Australia* bandsman Jack Richardson in September of the same year speaks with the fatalism of a committed supporter about his team's prospects in an upcoming game: 'We are going to play them at soccer, but I think they will win, and give us a hiding as they are the best band team in the Navy'.[307]

Farrier Bob Anderson, who played soccer for Moonyoonooka (outside Geraldton) before the war[308], was published in the *Geraldton Guardian* in March 1916.

> We have plenty of football (soccer).[309] We have formed a team out of this company, but it's the same old story only about half of us know the game. We have had three matches and haven't been beaten – two wins and a draw. Duncan got a team out of the 11th. He also got the old Queens Park centre (Swan) to play for them. He didn't play himself but he had a better football team than ours. However, it is not always the best team that wins, and they were very lucky to get a draw. They only scored in the last five minutes. Our goalkeeper thought the ball was going past, but it struck the post and went through. I was playing back and had plenty to do. I stopped Swan a few times. No doubt he is a good player and a dandy shot, but I think he is a bit rough. We will be playing next Saturday, so we may get knocked. I'm captain of this lot, and it's not too easy a job, as sometimes the best men either go to town (Cairo) or are out on duty. News is scarce, and a man can't say too much, as all letters are censored now. I met McPhie. He came over a week or ten days ago. I hope this finds all of you Geraldton boys in the pink. Give one and all my kindest regards. I'm afraid I won't be back in time for the football this season, so *au revoir*.[310]

Anderson indicates a flourishing soccer culture within the armed forces, even if not all of the participants were from soccer backgrounds. While Anderson complains that half do not know the rules, he might have rejoiced in the fact that half *did* know the rules.

Anderson's letter also raises the suggestion that the Australian teams are at least competitive. Lance-Corporal Gates reported that 'Our soccer football team lost to a team from an English regiment, by one goal to nil'.[311] Mr T Jones, YMCA secretary with the troops, 'who had both "Tommies" and "Kangaroos" in his charge' on the Sinai Peninsula, reiterates the familiarity many had with soccer. He wrote that 'Football matches are arranged about twice a week, both "Soccer and Rugby," and the excitement displayed is intense, and reminiscent of the old days at home'.[312]

In May 1916 Perth soccer journalist, Unomi wrote that he had:

> received letters from several soccerites on active service. Courcey O'Grady, Jimmie Cutmore, and Bert Shellat are all late officials of the J.B.F.A. They were all well at date of writing and desire to be remembered to their many soccer friends. Needless to add, they have been taking an active interest in football, particularly O'Grady and Cutmore who were members of an Egyptian team that did well in competition.[313]

This collection of letters suggests that there was an extensive and coordinated soccer program within the AIF.

As a whole the letters 'From the Front' reveal that soccer was available for Australian servicemen to play and/or observe – and they did one or the other, in their thousands. However, there are three tonalities in these letters: soccer subdominant, soccer neutral and soccer dominant. The vital question is of the extent to which Australian troops participated in soccer as a second-best to their preferred sport or as their preferred option.[314]

## SOCCER ENLISTMENTS

A significant and potentially contradictory point lost in the contemporary mythologisation of ANZAC is that many of those in the very first Australian troop ships were British-born, a good number of them recently arrived migrants. Cultural historian E M Andrews argues that the 'AIF had a large minority of British-born in it'. With pre-eminent military historian C E W Bean and other 'purveyors of the ANZAC legend' very much in his sights, Andrews suggests that a 'fact often overlooked' is that the British-born made up:

13.3 or 15.65 per cent of the Australian population, but
either 18 or 22.25 per cent of the AIF for the whole war,
depending on whose figures are taken. They were more
numerous in some formations, however, being 27 per cent
of the first contingent, and 50 per cent of the 28th Battalion,
from Perth . . . Whatever figures are accepted, the British-
born clearly volunteered in higher proportions than the
Australian-born, and considerably higher in the opening
days of the war.[315]

Bean accedes that many of those who enlisted were British-born but
suggests their relative numbers were severely whittled down prior to
embarkation. The following reads like a bad-faith rendering of statistics,
over-determined as it is by Bean's idea of the superiority of the Australian
bushman:

Since the only places for enlistment were in the capital
cities, many men had been recruited who would not
have been taken had the time been longer. The floating
population of these towns probably secured too large
a proportion of the acceptances. Immigrants from
Britain who happened to be about the cities showed an
extraordinary preponderance in the earlier stages – Colonel
MacLaurin left it on record that at one period 60 per cent
of the recruits for his brigade were British born; before it
sailed, 73 per cent of the men in the first contingent were
Australian born.[316]

And Bean suspects that many of the remainder would be as near
as good as Australian-born, their having 'lived in Australia since
childhood'.[317] It is not clear what Bean makes of the fact that of the first
58 to fall at Gallipoli (from the 11th Battalion) only just over half (31)
were Australian-born or had Australia-domiciled parents. Most of the
remainder were recently arrived, British-born, adult migrants.[318]

The widespread enlistment of British-born soldiers invites the
question of the percentage of the British-born enlistments who were also
soccer players, given the extent to which these migrants represented the

overwhelming majority of Australian soccer players. John Williamson's *Soccer Anzacs* tells the story of the Perth Caledonians' contribution to the war effort. It claims a direct nexus between the British-born, soccer and enlistment. Williamson claims that '300 players and officials enlisted from the WA soccer community and this is not surprising in light of the high proportion of Anzacs who were born in the United Kingdom'. It is possible that this figure sells WA soccer enlistments short.[319]

Exemplifying Williamson's point is the following excerpt from the *Daily News* in April 1915, prior to the Gallipoli landing:

> [The Perth YMCA] Soccer Club has responded splendidly to the call for men to serve our King and country abroad. By about the end of January the following members of the team had volunteered: Harry Amos, J. W. Balsdon, Herbert A. Bell, Frank M. Gill, James F. Jack, Cyril Jeans, J. S. Neale, A. Sage, Sid. Stubbs, P. Wrightson. Three are in Egypt, five are still in camp here, and two are waiting to be called up by the military authorities. The club is proud of the large number of soccer boys who have enlisted, and we are looking forward to seeing them return safe and sound. An interesting letter is to hand from Frank Gill, now in Egypt. He is fit and well, but anxious to get to the front. He says he has climbed the Pyramids.[320]

A willingness to enlist was a prevalent attitude found in soccer clubs in Western Australia and beyond – a commitment that had significant long-term ramifications for both the Caledonians Club and the game across Australia.

In October 1915, Unomi was able to report some astounding figures from Western Australia:

> The European war has played havoc with all winter pastimes, for every branch of sport has nobly responded to the country's call, and Westralian soccerites in particular have well maintained their name of sportsmen by giving of their best to the army at Gallipoli, as a glance at the list hereunder will testify. On looking back on the past year, the uppermost

feeling of the soccer community must be sadness with a measure of pride. Pride in the knowledge of the self-sacrifice made by many of our comrades in answering the appeal of the nation, and regret at the pitiless sacrifice of life. A number of those who were with us this time a year ago will no longer play the game. They fill honoured graves on the heights of Gallipoli, and much as I would like to write an appreciation of their courage and devotion of their country I do not feel equal to the task. From time to time the names of those players who enlisted have appeared in this column, it may therefore be fitting to give the number that has gone, or about to go, from each club. In doing so, however, it is not with any spirit of boastfulness, nor is it with the object of inviting comparisons, but in view of the somewhat disparaging statements made some time ago about football, I think it only my duty to show that soccer has done its bit and has nothing to reproach itself with. The list[321], which includes both associations, is:

| Club | Enlistments | Wounded | Killed |
|---|---|---|---|
| Austral | 17 | 4 | 1 |
| Caledonians | 7 | 0 | 0 |
| Casuals | 11 | 1 | 2 |
| Claremont | 46 | 3 | 4 |
| City Rangers | 13 | 3 | 3 |
| College | 25 | 4 | 3 |
| Fremantle | 6 | 0 | 1 |
| Perth | 14 | 1 | 6 |
| Referees | 7 | 1 | 2 |
| Thistle | 11 | 1 | 1 |
| Y.M.C.A. | 23 | 0 | 2 |
| Leederville | 11 | 0 | 1 |
| Other Clubs | 50 | 14 | 7 |
| Total | 241 | 32 | 33 |

On the resumption of soccer in Geraldton in 1919 Mr J G Scott, Hon. Secretary 'referred to the difficulties under which the last playing season, 1915, was concluded, owing to so many of the players going to the war, and which caused the game to be suspended the following seasons'. He ascertained that '62 of their players went to the front, and 16 of these had made the supreme sacrifice in defence of the Empire'.[322] In 1933 the president of the Geraldton Soccer Association revised these figures upward, claiming that 80 per cent of its players had enlisted. Of the 'just over one hundred players on the books of the Association', over eighty 'answered the great call and saw active service'.[323]

Like their WA brethren, soccer players across the country enlisted in droves, many of them prior to the Gallipoli campaign.

As discussed earlier, soccer had enjoyed a migrant-fuelled boom in pre-war Melbourne. Participation more than doubled between 1908 and 1912 and kept rising before the war. Harry Dockerty, the man most responsible for the game's Victorian regeneration, was not afraid to be boastful about the game he loved, so researchers must consider his statements on soccer participation carefully. He suggested at various points during the war that soccer's pre-war playing numbers were between 500 and 550. In October 1914 Melbourne sports newspaper the *Winner* went a little higher, claiming 597 registered players in the Victorian Amateur British Football Association.[324]

When it came to enlistments in the armed forces Dockerty had maintained in the early war period that around 40 per cent of Melbourne players had enlisted in the initial push while after the war much higher percentages were claimed. According to the *Argus*, at the first annual meeting of the British Association, on 16 June 1919 it was 'disclosed' that '90 per cent. of the players had enlisted for service abroad or at home. No competitive football had been played during the war'.[325]

Recent research has revealed that Dockerty's figures *were* inaccurate; but he was understating them! It is probably the case that there were more than 800 soccer players in Victoria in the pre-war period. A total figure of 1000 players is not out of the question.[326]

Despite the *Emerald Hill Record's* tendency to focus on Australian Rules footballers, it sometimes acknowledged the commitment of soccer players to the enlistment process. It reported the day before the Gallipoli invasion:

> Considerable difficulty has been experienced by the council
> of the 'Soccer' clubs in providing a satisfactory competition

for the forthcoming season, and it is only quite recently
that they have been able to draw up a complete fixture list.
As is generally known, the chief reason of this is the fact
that so many clubs have been hard hit by the large number
of players who have joined the Expeditionary Forces that it
has been extremely doubtful whether some of them would
be able to raise a team of any description.[327]

In July 1915 it reported (going so far as to break standard practice and
name individual soccer players) that more 'than a dozen players of the Thistle
club have joined the forces this week, and the senior team had to take the
field without the services of Goodson, Hogg, G. Brown, and Raitt'.[328] In
the growing consciousness of collective war interest, soccer as represented
by human personalities thus entered the mainstream Victorian press.

The Hobart *Mercury* recollected prior to the resumption of the inter-
state rivalry between Tasmania and Victoria in 1921: 'The last occasion
on which a Victorian team visited Tasmania was in August, 1914, and it
was at Hobart when war was declared. Seven of the team volunteered for
active service immediately on return to Melbourne'.[329]

In March 1915, the *Mercury* claimed that 'Soccer football stood out
as a fine example to all sporting organisations in Tasmania. The Elphin
Club had sent every one of its playing members to the war'.[330] Fifty
players from the top ten soccer clubs in Tasmania, north and south, had
enlisted by 1 April 1915.[331]

In South Australia player enlistments were also mounting. In April
1915 the Sturt Club reported losing 'the services of eight of last year's
players, who have enlisted in the Expeditionary Forces, and are now
in Egypt, but several new men having been secured the prospects are
bright'.[332]

While these departures were causing the game to wane, the clubs
'happily' sent their members off to the AIF with a sense of duty and pride,
as well as a semblance of propriety. The Adelaide Tramways team placed its
enlisted members in a prominent position in its 1914 team photo.

In Toowoomba (pop. 13,000 in 1914) the commitment was
remarkable. On the resumption of soccer in Toowoomba in 1919, at
'the annual meeting of the British Football Association it was reported
that 140 members of the association had gone to the Front'.[333]

British Football Club: Adelaide Tramways Company, 1914.
Courtesy of the State Library of South Australia.

In New South Wales the soccer enlistments were vast. Typical of the Sydney clubs, the Granville Magpies contributed heavily to the war effort. In total, 17 of 22 Magpie players in 1914 could 'be accounted for as having done or are doing their bit for King and country in foreign parts'.[334]

Australian soccer players were as keen as (if not more than) the players of other codes to do what they perceived as their duty. The next question is to ask is how well were the players 'embedded' in the mechanics of war? Were they *there*?

## SOCCER OVER THERE

For good or ill, Gallipoli is at the centre of the Australian story of sport and war. As the first major site of Australia's participation in the invasion of Turkey, it is commemorated as a tragic and courageous beginning of Australia's war campaign. As suggested earlier it is also a location for a powerful contemporary imagining of Australian nationality and cultural development. If 'ANZAC' can convey a general sense of Australian spirit, then 'Gallipoli' is the place of that spirit's founding.

**Soccer Match at Gallipoli, 1915.**
Courtesy of the Australian War Memorial.

And soccer was also at Gallipoli, and not merely in the actions of the soccer players (Allies and Australians) who fought and died there. It was played there. The above image of a soccer match being played at Gallipoli is the kind of picture that leaves little to be said. An organised game of soccer was played between Allied troops and they were being cheered on by hundreds of others. The game was conducted as part of the illusion that the Allies were carrying on as normal when in fact plans were being made to evacuate the Gallipoli Peninsula.[335]

While more evidence is needed to connect this visual image directly with Australian troops, they certainly played soccer on Lemnos in December 1915. Lemnos was loaned by Greece as a base 'for operations on the Gallipoli Peninsula'. An image collected by the Australian War Memorial shows members of the 6th Battalion playing there against a team from HMS *Hunter*. The men were likely en route to Egypt after participating in the Gallipoli campaign.

Former Geelong VFL footballer Leo Healy reported on his recuperation in Lemnos after having a tumour removed from his leg – resulting from

The team from the destroyer HMS *Hunter* playing against
a 6th Battalion team on the Aegean island of Lemnos in 1915.[336]
Courtesy of the Australian War Memorial.

an injury at Gallipoli. Healy described 'Lemnos as quiet, but the natural
harbour is beautiful. The men chiefly amuse themselves playing cricket
and Soccer football'.[337] Not only was soccer played at Gallipoli, it was
used as a means of refuge, recovery and relaxation by Australian troops in
the aftermath of the events that created the legend of ANZAC.

More symbolic evidence of the Australian game's intimate connection
with Gallipoli lies in the remarkable story of the soccer 'Ashes'. They
were conceived in 1923 during New Zealand's tour to Australia:

> Mr. Mayer (manager of the New Zealand soccer team)
> took back to the dominion the ashes in a box with a history
> attached to it. Mr. W. A. Fisher (secretary of the Queensland
> association) possessed a silver safety razor case presented to
> him when he left for the war, and it was with him when he
> landed with the Anzacs. He presented it to Mr. Mayer, and
> it contains some of the soil of Queensland and New South
> Wales, whose representatives played in the test matches. Mr.

> Mayer intends to have it mounted in New Zealand woods
> so that it may be a prized memento in connection with
> international matches between Australia and New Zealand.[338]

The 'Ashes' tag appeared to be a typical symbolic nod to the cricketing Ashes until it was revealed by the *Sydney Morning Herald* 13 years later that the case literally contained ashes.

> The 'Ashes,' incidentally, are a genuine trophy. They are a
> relic of the New Zealand team's visit to Australia 13 years
> ago, when the ashes of cigars smoked by the captains of the
> New Zealand and Australian team were placed in a plated
> safety-razor case, which, in turn, was enclosed in a casket
> of New Zealand and Australian timbers, honeysuckle and
> maple, suitably ornamented and inscribed. This trophy
> bears a record of the test games between the two countries
> since 1922, and was won three years ago by Australia,
> which beat the visiting New Zealand team in every test.[339]

The Sydney *Sun-Herald* reiterates the story of the Australia–NZ soccer 'Ashes' during the 1954 New Zealand tour of Australia:

> Ashes of two cigars, smoked in 1923, have become the
> Soccer Test 'Ashes,' won by Australia yesterday.
>
> The cigars were smoked at a Soccer dinner by the Australian
> captain, Alec Gibb, and the New Zealand captain, George
> Campbell, after New Zealand had won the 1923 Test series.
> They are contained in a silver safety razor case which was
> carried in the landing on Gallipoli by a New Zealand soldier.
>
> The razor case is set in a casket made of Australian and
> New Zealand woods inscribed with a kangaroo and the
> New Zealand fern leaf. The 'Ashes' were presented to the
> Australian team at a dinner in honour of the New Zealand
> side last night.[340]

Frequent test series over more than 30 years between the two ANZAC nations, playing for a trophy that 'witnessed' action at Gallipoli and is inscribed with powerful cultural icons, seems to be clear evidence of a deep and abiding relationship between soccer and the ANZAC story. Sports historian Richard Cashman wonders why this tradition died out in 1954 without ever stopping to marvel that it lasted as long as it did or to ponder the mechanics of its gestation.[341]

Indeed, this is a vital question because even as Australian soccer's quality, profile and professionalism were starting to rise in the 1950s, the game's connection with the *(Anglo-)Australian* past and its status within legend and mythology were undergoing erasure.

## CORNERS IN FOREIGN FIELDS

The final grisly question is what sort of toll did the fighting take on Australian soccer players? In May 1915 Unomi wrote ecumenically about the unfolding tragedy of the war and its impact on local soccer in Perth:

> At the great match now raging in the Dardanelles the enemy is no respecter of codes. It is all the same to them whether their bullets find billets in an adherent of the Australian, Rugby or Soccer games. Therefore, with so many of our players at the front British Associationists must expect to contribute towards the blood toll now being exacted. That we are doing so is evidenced in the fact that since the declaration of war no less than five have passed hence. Two, Private Courtney and Major Parker through illness, and three in action – namely Private Amos (Referees' Association), Major Carter (Perth Club), and Private Algy Hale (Claremont Glebe). At the usual meeting of the association on Wednesday last, reference was made to the loss sustained, and a motion to the effect that letters of condolence be sent to the relatives of the deceased was passed. Amongst those reported on the injury list is Lieutenant Rockliffe. Old timers will remember Mr. Rockliffe as being the first secretary of the Junior Association and also a great enthusiast in schools football. I am sure every soccerite will wish him a speedy recovery.[342]

Ultimately, the most powerful (and harrowing) evidence of soccer's 'being there' lies in the bodies of the men who stayed there, those who died in the carnage. When the Toowoomba British Football Association regathered in 1919 they noted their own toll:

> During the evening the Chairman extended a hearty
> welcome home to the returned men present, and Mr.
> S. Morgan responded on behalf of the returned men.
> The secretary stated that the British Football Association
> ('Soccer') was the only football association that had an
> honour roll in Toowoomba. The names of Syd. Cousens,
> Lit. Groom, A. Dundas[ch], Colin Groom, W. Bury, and
> J. McManus were recorded in the minutes as having paid
> the supreme sacrifice in the late Great War.[343]

Pre-war soccer had not only grown in the metropolitan and larger regional centres. As the previous chapter discussed, it had taken root in the country as well. Centres and towns like Broken Hill, Rockhampton, Charters Towers and Warwick had established bustling soccer cultures that were all inevitably truncated by the war effort.

Mildura, too, had a developing competition in this period. Even when soccer was in decline in Melbourne in the 1890s, Mildura had kept the flag flying for a few years, engaging in local scratch matches and playing irregular competition with South Australian town, Renmark. The Mildura competition before the war involved two or three teams. While Merbein dropped in and out, the Mildura and Irymple clubs kept up a steady battle for the four years between 1911 and 1915. Made up of many British migrants but, perhaps unusually, also many native-born, the competition was a passionate little outpost of Victorian soccer, cruelly interrupted by the war. Not cruel because it interrupted a sports competition; that is merely unfortunate. But cruel because of the damage it inflicted on a community.

Tiny Irymple, Mildura's satellite settlement, was ravaged by the war. The fate of its soccer players is only a part of the larger tale of horror. The Irymple team photograph is like many other shots of this kind. It captures a team of fit young men, probably friends, revealing pride and comradeship. They knew

Irymple Soccer Team, 1913
Back Row - E. Leach, R. McCune, R. Brown. Centre - D. Morrison, N. Holmes, I. Mallock.
Front - J. Goodman, R. Campbell, P. Beckett, A. Stevens, J. Campbell.

Above: Irymple Soccer Team, Mildura, 1913.
Below, postcard appended to the photograph.
Courtesy of the Mildura Rural City Council Library Service.

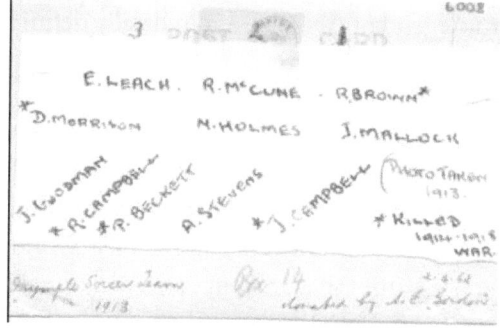

little of the horror to come. A postcard appended to the photograph by its donor in 1962 acknowledges that five of the players (the ones asterisked) were killed in the war.

Sadly, even this horrific figure does not reveal the full extent of the truth. The club actually lost nine (possibly even ten) of its members. To this extent it may well be the Australian soccer club that lost more players at the war than any other. The following are the Irymple dead:

Percy Hamlin Beckett *
R Brown *
Jas Campbell *
R F Campbell *
Jack Hart
David Lindsay Morrison *
William Jefferies
Robert Samuel Page
Thomas Edwin Surgey
A B Wadham (either he or his brother played soccer for
Irymple)

Like many clubs in many sports across rural Australia, members enlisted
with gusto. Fate was to decree which battalions they joined and casualties
were often determined by the luck of the draw. Some communities ended
up being more unlucky than others in the way their volunteers were
channelled into particularly devastating theatres and campaigns of war.
The Irymple nine were indeed visited with a terrible fate.

The scale of this tragedy is nearly matched by the example of the
Caledonian team in Perth. Eight members of the club (six first-team
players) lost their lives in active service. John Williamson, author of *Soccer
Anzacs*, concludes his book by making a claim for soccer's centrality in
the legend of ANZAC and radically defining Australian heritage in terms
of actions and commitment rather than birthplace:

> Few sporting clubs in Australia were so decimated in
> the War's bloody battles as the Caledonian Soccer Club.
> Practically every player and official enlisted and served under
> the Australian flag in the First World War. They took part in
> battles that are remembered throughout Australia every year
> on 25th April – battles burnt into the Australian psyche.
>
> These Caledonians were Anzacs and what started off as a Scottish
> strand was woven into the fabric of Australia society by the deeds
> of its gallant youth. If we reflect on the sacrifice of this team
> we realise that it paid in blood for the right to use the name
> Caledonians and be accepted as part of our Australian heritage.[344]

## A GAP 'IN THE RECORD'

Australian soccer historians rarely write about the First World War. It is usually a mere break in their narrative. Yet as I hope I have shown it needs to be far more than that. It is, firstly, the place of another dislocated kind of rich soccer history that reveals a game far more central to Australian stories than has been hitherto acknowledged. Australians played and observed games of soccer during the war and many were newly introduced to the game solely because of their participation in the war. Secondly, the war is that which prevents, perhaps more than any other force, the game's then seemingly inevitable rise to a degree of prominence across Australia. After the war, with more migrants and with renewed enthusiasm, soccer set off once more on its merry course of rebuilding. But this time the enemies within the other football codes were forewarned and forearmed.

The migrants of the 1920s were greater in number but perhaps lesser in commitment to spreading the 'British game of football'. History was once more unkind[345] and, despite the seemingly better organised streams of migration, it is not until after the Second World War that the kind of ferocious passion for soccer generated by a migrant boom is seen again.[346] This 30-year break might well be the great developmental blockage for the game of soccer in Australia. The elision of soccer and its British-born adherents in the construction of the Australian legend of the First World War was a significant factor in this limit to soccer's growth.

# CHAPTER 7

# FROM DÉTENTE TO DISTRUST

In 1931 soccer authorities in Hobart sought access to the North Hobart football ground, normally reserved for Australian Rules. They requested its use for representative games on the two days of the season when it was not needed by the Southern Tasmanian [Australian Rules] Football Association for first-grade matches. Typically there were expressions of resistance to this desire, one of which was a letter to the *Mercury* penned by 'Derwentside'. He argued that:

> 'Soccer' players and followers in Hobart are in a minority
> only a self-centred, and, which is worse, a selfish, player
> or supporter, would deny. Whatever merits 'Soccer' has
> as a winter game, it has not here the following, status, or
> genuine sportsman-like appeal to the average Australian
> as the game which some fifty odd years has evolved under
> the name of Australian football. The proper development
> of a nation's national pastimes, particularly the winter
> ones, does more to build up a virile nation than attempts
> to foster – or is it foist? – an exotic pastime upon them.
> Among the many thousands of Australians who manned
> so doggedly the trenches and trudged the fields of France
> and Flanders – to say nothing of the Gallipoli campaign
> – not a small percentage got the qualities which made the
> A.I.F. world renowned from the fields in at least four States
> devoted in winter to football played under Australian
> Rules.[347]

This is one more letter published in relation to one more moment in the interminable squabble for playing space in Australian sport. And it articulates many of the sentiments that had come to take hold in the Australian sports imaginary: soccer is low, unpopular, unestablished, minor, foreign ('exotic' in fact) and is being imposed/foisted on Australians by selfish and self-centred agents of foreign influence.[348]

The letter also raises an interesting and new basis for exclusion. 'Derwentside' claims that Australian Rules supplied many of the troops who fought in the First World War and his necessary implication is the lie that soccer did not. Accordingly, Australian Rules should have prior claim on whatever sports fields over which it has established patterns of usage. Australian Rules paid for this access with the blood, sweat and sometimes the lives of many of its adherents who enlisted in the AIF. While an invalid argument, it has been a persuasive one, ever since it was first concocted.

Four years earlier, in 1927, a letter to the editor of the *Sunshine Advocate* in Melbourne also invoked the ANZAC spirit. 'Dinkum Aussie'[349] complained:

> It was stated by two returned soldiers, and reported in your
> paper, that an attempt is being made by some Johnny-Come-
> Latelys to supplant our national game of football with an
> importation. On making inquiry, I find that a local school
> teacher is working might and main against the national
> game, and I am told that at least one of the local soccer team
> is an Australian. I should like to suggest that the local football
> club report the matter to the head office in town, so that
> it may be brought before the Minister. If Victoria is good
> enough to live in, its games should be good enough to play.[350]

Many of the usual tropes are deployed: the national is game being supplanted by a 'Johnny-come-lately'. The 'when-in-Rome' argument is invoked. And those pesky 'Pommy' schoolteachers are up to their usual tricks.[351] Moreover, we get a hint of treachery insofar as an 'Australian' lad has been tempted into tasting the forbidden fruit. Amplifying this is the prefatory fact that it was two returned soldiers who reported it, as if their being moved to comment proves the outrage.

Both writers suggest that soccer was a marginal game in post-war Australia. Moreover, it can be inferred that they think it is a game with very little to do with the ANZAC history or spirit. A vital question is the extent to which the sentiments expressed by 'Derwentside' and 'Dinkum Aussie' represented significant popular thought and the extent to which they have stuck in Australian cultural memory. These sentiments are nonetheless indicative of the long historical failure of soccer to embed itself as a component of the national cultural-mythological discourse, especially when it comes to military history.

Immediately after the First World War soccer had acquired a small but secure place in Melbourne sports culture. Soccer's commitment to the war effort gave its adherents the *basis* for entry into the formation of a new national mythology. Increasing migrant numbers in the 1920s swelled the number of soccer's participants and supporters. Perhaps counter-intuitively, this growth was accompanied by an increasing distance between the game and notions of Australianness. This chapter traces the cooling of soccer's welcome in Melbourne between 1920 and 1934 to the point where the game was cast to the margins of Australian identity.

## ONLY IN MELBOURNE

Perhaps only in Melbourne does a brooding, hidebound and monolithic structure of feeling dominate, where other codes are sometimes humoured and usually dismissed as inferior. Yet even this attitude softened from time to time. Melbourne's press was sometimes faintly supportive of soccer after a few initial warning shots in the early 1880s.[352] In the period immediately following the First World War, the press and the VFL seemed to take a positive attitude to soccer, a game that had contributed so much to the war effort that it and its players were impossible to forget so quickly. Too many soccer players had appeared in Rolls of Honour for their efforts to be dismissed as marginal. It appears that in 1920 soccer belonged as a small but significant component of Melbourne sports culture.

While soccer's contribution to the ANZAC story has been largely forgotten today, it was hard to escape in the immediate post-war period. Soccer's commitment to the war effort was often noted in the press. In 1920 the *Argus* reported that the very strong Northumberland and

Durhams club were 'popularly known as the "all-digger" team'.[353] The very first post-war England v Scotland international, in 1920, was well promoted in the press as a post-war event and attracted a sizeable crowd of between 5000 and 6000.[354] Even as late as 1927 a suburban soccer match memorialising ANZAC was being promoted by the press.[355]

What follows is a series of moments and case studies that trace a changing attitude towards soccer in Melbourne and the rebuilding of the ideology that soccer is a 'wicked foreign game'.[356]

## SOCCER AT THE MCG, 1920

In 1920 the VFL momentarily invited soccer into the fold, allowing the game a promotional opportunity before a large crowd at the MCG. A match between the crew of the royal yacht *Renown* and a Victorian selection was played as a curtain raiser to an inter-state Australian Rules match on 29 May. 'It is a fascinating game to watch when played by high-class performers,' read one preview in the VFL's *Football Record*:

> It is as nearly as possible pure football, only the goalkeepers being permitted to intentionally handle the ball. Even they have to drop it like a hot potato. Dribbling is something that will cause wonder to those who have never seen the game. It is the working of the ball along the ground with the foot. Another bit of business that calls for good judgment is the 'heading'– meeting the ball with the head and directing it off the block in some particular direction. I wonder if the term, 'Using his block,' was derived from this.[357]

The game day *Football Record* indeed delivered on its promise, providing a useful guide to some points of the game and player information.

The previews are couched in the assumptions implicit in the relationship between a local culture and what is understood as a foreign game. They presume an extent to which local readers will be confused by what they see and repeat the assumption of ignorance whereby the spectators are constructed as knowing nothing about soccer. Nonetheless, the previews are voluble and positive. While soccer is not seen as a threat to the 'Australian' game or to local culture, this kind of generosity of spirit is possible from both the VFL and the press. It is the generosity of a comfortable host.

Five years later the mood had changed. In the meantime Australian Rules authorities had grown increasingly restive through observations of soccer's migrant-fuelled growth around Melbourne and country Victoria. One simple indicator had been identified: the massive growth in soccer-ball production. In response to this the VFA urged that steps be taken to ensure the VFL obtained tenure over the 'Amateur Sports Ground'.[358] The *Argus* reported:

> The British Association game is growing so rapidly that it is anxious to secure headquarters . . . As an indication of the growth of the British Association ('Soccer'), it may be mentioned that last year 40 gross (5760) of 'soccer' balls were manufactured in Melbourne. This year the total is 144 gross (20,736), and clubs have been established in various country centres. In view of these three bodies having cast eyes on the Amateur Sports ground, the League may find that it must have this ground, and that the way out is the inclusion of the public service team.[359]

Rather than allow the 'foreign code' to obtain an enclosed ground as its headquarters in Melbourne, some Australian Rules authorities saw the need to exclude soccer from this kind of belonging, even if it meant scrambling together a new football club drawing on players from the public service without the kind of suburban base on which the successful clubs were built.[360] Something was happening somewhere and, despite the fact that the authorities did not quite know what it was, the host's generosity was diminished and the spirit of cooperation appeared to be buckling.

## SOCCER AT THE MCG, 1925

In 1925 an English FA team toured Australia. In another example of its capacity for courtesy and generosity, the VFL happily cooperated to allow a soccer 'Test match'[361] to go ahead on its premier ground, the

MCG while the Melbourne (Australian Rules) FC first team was playing away.

But this spirit was not general. The VFL's sister organisation, the SA Football League, had refused to allow an international game between Australia and England to be played at the Adelaide Oval in late April.

A mere five years after warmly welcoming soccer to the MCG, the *Football Record* felt moved to scorn, observing that Australian Rules 'has little to fear from the soccer' after 'seeing the Englishmen play against a Victorian team' on Wednesday 20 May 1925. In language that recalls many of the comments from Australian-Rules-playing soldiers in their letters from the Front, Danny Minogue, the Richmond captain, claimed after the game: 'There is not one point in their game that could not be quickly adapted by Australian Rules players if necessary, but there are many finer things in our game which make it far more spectacular and faster'. The *Record* went on to claim:

> Wels Eicke, Horry Clover, Dave McNamara and others who were present agreed with Dan. As a thrilling game, with wonderfully fine spectacular incidents throughout, OUR game stands alone. Neither soccer nor Rugby can come within cooee of it.[362]

Perhaps Australian Rules did have little to fear from what was seen on the pitch. A second-string England team was not tested by the Victorian XI. The *Record* failed to account for the reasons for the mismatch. Nor did it note the 7–0 score line. However, it also failed to mention something that might well have caused a little disquiet in VFL ranks. The crowd for the game was a respectable 5600. The receipts were a more than respectable £463, a figure that at the time would have represented good takings at a well-attended VFL match.

These numbers must have confounded the Melbourne journalists, whose local soccer coverage was usually meagre. Given the loyalist underpinnings of the only superficially nationalistic Melbourne press, the arrival of a British team with royalty (via the Earl of Stradbroke, Governor of Victoria) in tow had forced their hands somewhat. The article appearing in the *Argus* on the morning of the game was extensive and included an explanatory diagram.[363]

This level of coverage was maintained for the subsequent 'Test' between Australia and England, at the same venue on Saturday 23 May. It conveys a sense of the journalist previewing the game having had to brush up very quickly on his soccer information. The *Argus* writer has trouble coming to grips with the transition from the idea of the Victorian state team to the Australian national team and demonstrates little practical or local knowledge of Australian soccer:

> Both England and Australia have made seven changes in the teams that will meet at the Melbourne Cricket ground this afternoon. Robison (goal-keeper), Aiken, Ritchie, and Orr (who played on Wednesday) the only men who retain their position in the Australian team, the new members being Maunders and McNaughton (from New South Wales), Mitchell (from South Australia), Honeysett (from Tasmania), and Bristow, W. Raitt, and Morrison (of Victoria). The side will be much strengthened by these changes.

The report goes on to list the England changes before concluding that 'His Excellency the Governor the Earl of Stradbroke will kick off at 3 o'clock'.[364]

The *Argus* also assumed, as was typical, that many of its readers would be as bemused as themselves by the game, so it supplied an adequate description of the game, including a serviceable attempt at explaining the offside rule.[365]

Despite the relatively large attendance for the weekday warm-up game, the authorities had underestimated the demand for the upcoming 'Test' match on the Saturday, possibly because they did not comprehend the step up from state to national representation. It is equally possible that they felt that, with the game going head-to-head with VFL and VFA football, a small crowd was likely. In the event, it seems that too few turnstiles were in operation and many spectators were unable to enter the stadium until very close to game time. Press reports were thankful of the fact that many of the crowd were English migrants and so queued in an orderly fashion.[366]

The photographic focus of the *Argus* seemed very much on the English side of things. It published an image of the English team meeting the

Earl of Stradbroke before the game and another photograph of a group of English sailors enjoying themselves at the game.

The game went ahead successfully and was won quite easily by England, 5–0. However, events off the field made it a watershed moment in Victorian football history.

First, a large crowd of 10,600 had been registered for a soccer match in Melbourne at the home of Australian Rules football. Even more telling than the crowd numbers were the receipts – which more than doubled those of any simultaneously held VFL game.[367] The crowd had paid £995 to get in, a phenomenal figure for one game. The *Argus*[368] reported these receipts in comparison with the figures for the weekend fixtures across the two local Australian Rules competitions:

### 'SOCCER.'

| | | |
|---|---|---|
| England v. Australia | 10, 600 | £995 |

**League**

| | | |
|---|---|---|
| Richmond v. South Melbourne | 22,000 | £430 |
| St. Kilda v. Fitzroy | 17,000 | £415 |
| Collingwood v. Geelong | 16,000 | £375 |
| North Melbourne v. Essendon | 15,000 | £350 |
| Footscray v. Melbourne | 12,000 | £290 |
| Carlton v. Hawthorn | 10,000 | £230 |
| Total | 92,000 | £2,060 |

**Association**

| | | |
|---|---|---|
| Coburg v. Brunswick. | 7,000 | £126 |
| Northcote v. Port Melbourne | 4,000 | £56 |
| Geelong v. Williamstown | 2,000 | £40 |
| Brighton v. Prahran | 2,000 | £27 |
| Total | 15,000 | £249 |

One game of soccer took in four times the VFA's total receipt figures (figures that were boosted no doubt by the Sydney Road 'derby' between Coburg and Brunswick) and one-half of the VFL's total figure. While the quality of the game and even the relatively large crowd were nothing to remark upon, the gate takings set alarm bells ringing. 'Soccer's money' (via rich investors and globalisation) is a notion that still has valency. Perhaps this game was the first time that idea was embodied in hard cash in Victoria. The *Sporting Globe* certainly reported the tour as successful both culturally and financially.[369]

The rhetoric of the Melbourne football press shifted during the first half of the 1920s from a position based in beneficent fairness and equanimity to a slightly bemused and assertive advocacy of Australian Rules over the foreign, British codes. The dominant structure of feeling that had shown signs of weakening in the immediate post-war period was by 1925 reasserting itself. Within a two further years elements of the sports press were to become the VFL's attack dogs, savaging soccer as a matter of course if not policy.

## SOCCER AT THE FITZROY CRICKET GROUND, 1911–1927

Until 1986 the Fitzroy Cricket Ground (known popularly today as Brunswick Street Oval) was the summer home of its lessee, Fitzroy Cricket Club. It was also the home of the Fitzroy [Australian Rules] Football Club until 1966. Fitzroy FC sub-leased the ground from the cricket club each winter until tensions over rental between the two clubs reached breaking point. While notionally a cricket ground, the oval was, in terms of revenue and attendance, primarily an Australian Rules football ground.

The Fitzroy Cricket Ground also hosted many high-level soccer matches in its history. First-Division, Dockerty Cup, inter-state matches, and 'local' and 'genuine' international matches were often held at Fitzroy in the early part of the twentieth century. Many attracted substantial crowds, the biggest of which was the 12,000 that turned up to watch the touring Chinese team in 1923.

The first organised soccer match on the ground was the local so-called 'international' between teams representing 'Scotland' and 'England' on 12 August 1911.[370] Matches between English- and Scottish-born players

Scotland v England at the Fitzroy Cricket Ground, 10 August 1912.
Courtesy of the Melbourne *Leader*.

in Melbourne represent a significant tradition in early Melbourne soccer going back to 13 September 1884 with the first 'international' being played in Albert Park. These games were relocated to the Fitzroy Cricket Ground in 1911 and were last played there in 1926.

The above image is from the Melbourne *Leader* of 17 August 1912. It depicts the 1912 match that was won 3–0 by Scotland. The crowd for the 1912 game is not mentioned, but the photograph suggests a sizeable turnout. The *Queensland Times* reported the crowd as between 6000 and 7000.[371] A year later the *Argus* claimed a crowd of 4000 attended the 1913 game. Using these figures and the image as evidence, it might be assumed that somewhere above 4000 is a 'normal' crowd for the Melbourne soccer community's game of the season – though the purported 1921 attendance of nearly 9000 should warn against underestimation. From 1928 the games were played at the Motordrome.

As lessee, the Cricket Club was one of the main beneficiaries of the gate receipts.[372] Why it would end or allow the ending of such a financially beneficial relationship is not made explicit in the press. Pressure from the Australian Rules community was an important factor.

The following is an excerpt from a May 1927 piece in the *Argus* entitled 'Rival Code Seeks League Ground'. It outlines the objection made by the VFL to Fitzroy Cricket Club (FCC) continuing to rent their ground out to soccer bodies. Even though it meant losing income, the cricket club yielded to the pressure. The reference to the 'old trouble' suggests that this was not the first time it had been an issue:

'We have the old trouble again,' said Mr. V. J. McDonnell, secretary of the League second eighteens, 'for the Fitzroy Cricket Club has asked the Fitzroy seconds to vacate the ground on June 25 and July 9 for an international soccer game. We understood that we had the ground for the season.'

Mr. M. E. Green (Fitzroy delegate) said that the cricket club had full power to let the ground, except when the seniors were using it. He understood that the cricket club had arranged another ground for the seconds, and intended to compensate them

Mr. F. Reid (Essendon) said it was 'the thin edge of the wedge' in an effort to introduce a different code of football. The seconds were of very great assistance to the seniors, and the grounds should not be taken away from them

Mr. McDonnell said that the Fitzroy seconds would benefit financially by going off the ground on the dates required, but were thinking of the good of the game.

Mr. D. Crone (Carlton) considered that strong objection should be taken to any League ground being leased to soccer or rugby football.

Mr. L. H. McBrien (South Melbourne) moved that the League write to the Fitzroy Cricket Club and the Grounds' Management Association to the effect that the League viewed with alarm the suggested action of the Fitzroy Cricket Club in proposing to let the ground for the use of a foreign code to the detriment of the Australian game. In seconding the motion, which was agreed to, Mr. Reid said the Australian game, and not soccer, was the source of the revenue obtained by the grounds.[373]

The post-war détente in which soccer was seen as a small but nonetheless domesticated game was clearly over if the intensity of this report is any indication. Soccer resumed its 'wicked foreign' status.

Even though the Cricket Club had 'made arrangements' and found an alternative ground for FFC's second 18, it was still subjected to pressure by the VFL, which requested that 'a clause be inserted in the agreement that the ground be available for the Australian game during the whole of the season'. An *Argus* report, under the baldly propagandist subheading, 'Resisting Foreign Code' intimates the extent to which FCC were forced into a submissive position:

> At the ordinary meeting that followed further reference to the action of the Fitzroy Cricket Club in allowing a soccer match on a Saturday, which meant that the [FFC] second 18 had to make other arrangements, was made when the Fitzroy Club wrote that the arrangements had been made between the bodies concerned, and there was no intention on its part to foster a foreign code.[374]

Despite VFL objections, the 1927 Chinese game against Australia went ahead, attracting a smallish crowd on a miserable day. The income that attendance generated for FCC was the last it would obtain from the 'foreign code' because soccer appears immediately to have been exiled from the ground. Soccer's 16-year tenure at Fitzroy and the England v Scotland game's 40-year local history counted for nothing in the haste to evict an alien invader from the ground and, in some cases, from its historiography.[375]

## COLLAPSE

In 1927 it appeared that soccer might take off as a major sport in Victoria. It was expanding rapidly on the back of migration and starting to work its way into popular consciousness – as the sometimes sizeable crowds attest. The media even began to take notice. The *Sporting Globe* handed the game over to a permanent member of staff for the first time in 1928 and the *Argus* and the *Age* ran reasonably wide coverage.[376]

Australian Rules authorities were also starting to worry about the threat of soccer, once more mobilising the rhetorical tropes of opposition constructing soccer as a foreign, invasive and feeble game and practically opposing its expansion via their contacts and influence in the councils. Its organ, the *Football Record*, took up an at times stridently propagandist role for Australian Rules and occasionally took direct aim at the 'British codes' of soccer and rugby.

As seems soccer's way, however, such gains were to be confounded by a customary periodic collapse – only this time self-inflicted. The game shot itself in the foot through a split in both New South Wales and Victoria. In Victoria, a proposal to organise the competition on a district or suburban basis led to some clubs breaking away to form their own organisation. The 'breakaway Melbourne and Metropolitan District Association battled with the established Melbourne and District Association during the 1927 and 1928 seasons' thereby taking the not insubstantial wind out of the game's sails.[377]

The Victorian schism had just been mended in March 1929 when economic depression compounded the self-administered problems. Attendances remained small and clubs struggled to establish bases in their local communities. By 1936, the competition had declined to two divisions – eight teams in Division One and nine in Division Two – and a junior competition and a schools competition for the Dunkling Cup. The 'international' and inter-state matches continued, and international touring teams arrived at irregular intervals, but the basis for the optimism of the late 1920s had long since evaporated.

To understand this ongoing tendency of soccer to snatch derision from the jaws of acclamation, both internal divisions and external pressures acting upon the game need to be accounted for. It will not do to see the game's progress as being hindered or boosted by actions of only one or the other force. It can only be understood as a result of a dialectical or dance-like relationship with move and counter-move, step and counter-step, claim and counter-claim being the pattern – occasional stepped-on toes, clumsy collisions and ill-mannered cutting-in providing momentary relief from the tedium of it all.

Even as Victorian soccer entered the 1930s in a sorry state the VFL press remained wary of the threat the game had represented in the mid- to late 1920s, taking every opportunity to remind its readers what a weak and passionless game soccer was. In a truly astounding piece of journalism, the VFL saw fit to publish editor G. Cathie's withering epistolary account of English soccer in its 1934 Grand Final edition of the *Football Record*.[378] 'Australian Game Vastly Superior' is a fabricated (if not delusional) reminder for readers that Australian Rules is truly the only game for Australia:

Some interesting and illuminating comments on the soccer code of football as played in England, compared with our own Australian game, is contained in a letter received this week from Mr G Cathie, a life member of the League, who is at present in England. The letter runs as follows:—

'Whilst in Newcastle I saw the opening match of the soccer season and to say I was disappointed is to put it very mildly. Believe me, soccer is not in the same street as our game and it made me feel proud to belong to an organisation that plays the Aussie code. There was little enthusiasm amongst the crowd, which numbered about 14,000, and the deliberate 'kicking-out' was atrocious and a blot on their game.

'The full backs are the only players allowed to touch the ball with their hands, and they are afraid, when in possession, to leave the goal by more than 15 yards. Then they punt the ball with a kick which as often as not goes in the opposite direction to where it is intended. What salaries would await some of our Aussie rules full backs if they were to come over here.

'They could learn all there is in the code in a week or two, and would become champions in a month!

'Think of players like Jack Regan, Frank Gill, Maurie Heahan, Ron Hillis, 'Jacka' Todd, Jack Vosti, and Bill Tymms and Bert Hyde in their prime, coming out with the ball from the goal mouth like a streak of lightning, vigorous, pacy, spectacular – and generally with only one man to pass. Then footing the ball to the other end – it would create a sensation in England. If we could only teach our English cousins the great charm and exhilaration of our national sport, it would be wonderful.'

The article claims that soccer is an inferior game for a number of reasons. It is less exciting and exhilarating. The crowd numbers are low and those who attend are not enthusiastic towards the game. The players are afraid to be adventurous and they are incompetent at what they do.

The writer assumes (like Jack Dyer after him)[379] that with a little bit of training VFL footballers would take soccer by storm. Ultimately, Cathie's complaint is simply that soccer is guilty of the crime of not being Australian Rules football.

Significantly, the letter shifts mood midstream. Having started out as a hard-nosed and prejudiced critique of soccer's faults, it suddenly transforms into a fantasy of Australian Rules internationalism. Coveting the salaries of the English game for Australian Rules champions and regretting the refusal of 'English cousins' to be taught the merits of his game, Cathie's piece becomes a resentful hymn to the game's failure to belong anywhere beyond the southern half of Australia. Beneath the triumphalism lies a xenophobia scored into the psyches of large swathes of Australian sports culture.

It seems unnecessary to go beyond one word – 'silly' – to summarise the article. However, when it is realised that the author is inventing material as well as leaving out crucial information then the piece shifts from the realms of silliness to propaganda. Cathie can be forgiven for calling the goalkeepers full-backs (Victorian Rules full-backs were at one time referred to as goalkeepers), but he can't be forgiven for calling them cowardly for refusing to handle the ball illegally outside of the penalty area. Yet the more serious errors are ones of detail. The author claims to have gone to the opening game of the season (25 August) in the Newcastle area. Problematically, Newcastle United were playing away on this day, hammered 5–1 by Nottingham Forest. The professional teams in the area who played at home on that day were Gateshead and Darlington (division three) and first-division Sunderland, which beat Huddersfield Town 4–1 at Roker Park – a game at which there were almost 30,000, a few more than 14,000.[380]

However, accuracy in reporting was not at the forefront of the writer's mind. The important work to be done on Grand Final day 1934 was simply to remind Australian Rules spectators that soccer was an illegitimate and uninspiring game compared with what they were about to receive, fare that deserved to be served to the world. The great tragedy of such propaganda is that in the 1930s there was almost no contradictory source of qualitative information on English football for readers of the *Football Record*. Such dishonest propaganda therefore found easy entry into the realm of 'truth' for generations of Victorian football aficionados and the stories they held and repeated.

The effect of this propaganda cannot be underestimated historically or politically. The process creates collective or social memory grounded in historical exclusion, marginalisation and untruth. Such social memory becomes an important tool for cultural-political elites to enhance legitimacy and control. In this way hegemony is achieved or solidified. The stories told about soccer in the name of the VFL are very much part of this process of maintaining cultural hegemony. While the dominance of Australian Rules football at this time is not in question, the lies it tells itself and its supporters about the world of sport point to a severe case of anxiety and insecurity.

The most important aspect of this propaganda work is the reaffirmation of the notion of soccer as a foreign game, an issue soccer still confronts 90 years later. In 1920 in Melbourne soccer was a perfectly legitimate local option for those so inclined to play the game, in such suburbs as Albert Park, Coburg, Preston, Footscray and others. Soccer had a brief window of opportunity in the 1920s to establish itself as a legitimately Australian game in Victoria. That window closed quickly under the manifold pressures of VFL's political influence, its nationalistic and xenophobic propaganda, economic depression and soccer's self-inflicted turmoil. It has never fully reopened.

# CONCLUSION

Australian soccer has so many powerful and noble stories to tell. This book has explored and scratched the surface of just a few of them: the deep history of round-ball, non-handling football in Australia; the popularity of soccer in Perth in the early 1900s; soccer spotfires across rural Australia prior to the First World War; the soccer ANZACs; and the robust strength of soccer in Melbourne in the mid-1920s. Each could (and probably will) represent subject matter for further book-length studies.

Each narrative is couched here in a context of cultural neglect and dismissal if not outright opposition and antagonism. Soccerphobia has been identified as a vital accompaniment to each of the stories whether manifested through direct confrontation, backroom political manoeuvres, media bias, activism and incompetence, or surveillance from a distance.

This context has been a vital limiter to the game's sense of legitimacy and belonging. As an illegitimate alien, soccer has been detained for questioning by customs and its right to remain silent has been turned into an obligation. Its stories have been noted and 'misplaced' in the wrong filing cabinet. Its dream of flourishing untrammelled in Australia has been undermined by forces of myopic cultural nationalism and xenophobia, variously offended by the game's 'inferiority' and difference, and afraid of its assumed global power. Soccer has been excluded from the norms and values inscribed in national cultural memory and the 140-year history of the organised game in Australia counts for little or nothing in its endeavours to sit alongside other cultural pastimes as an equal.

This book, in focusing on the forces of amnesia and rejection, has unapologetically constructed a narrative of repression that will be absent in other histories that strive for 'balance' in telling the stories of soccer's travails. While repression is not the whole story of soccer in Australia, it is a necessary component in any full understanding of how the game that became the world's obsession remains such a poor relation in Australia. I leave it to other writers and other times to blame soccer for its own abjection. They have a point, but it is not one I have wanted to make here.

Focusing on repression has also lent a sense of inevitability to the forgetfulness that the game endures. To keep a culture down it is necessary to strip it of its memories and prevent its access to the means of recording its history. Yet there was and is nothing inevitable about the vanishing history of Australian soccer. Human agency and human practice are such that stories will be remembered and passed down to later generations even in the most difficult of circumstances. So it has been with Australian soccer. Our present task is to find, research and broadcast these stories and create a wealth of public history that will cast out forever the great lie that soccer is the game that never happened in Australia.

This is the problem around which this book has turned: Australian soccer has failed to rise to the level of mythology, legend and story in Australia. Soccer historians Philip Mosely and Bill Murray put it another way: 'it has not entered the Australian soul'.[381] Hay claims that 'there has been a failure to make the game Australian.'[382] It has not managed to insert itself positively into the narratives that Australians tell themselves about themselves. This is the basis upon which it is possible to utter the patent falsity that Australian soccer is the game that never happened.

Even though there continue to be countless moments of individuals, teams and organisations *seeming* to play and organise soccer matches and competitions, the game has never *really* happened in and for itself. It has been an *instead* game and a *nearly* game, a counter-attraction or curtain-raiser to the main game wherever and whenever it has been played. Australians have played and watched soccer as a digression, a replacement, a substitute, a surrogate, a next-best thing at best, when they would rather be doing something else, somewhere else.

So games of soccer that were very much played, and won (or drawn) did not 'happen' in the sense that they did not register as significant moments of *Australian* behaviour. Like mirages, they appeared on the horizon and vanished as suddenly as they emerged not even to be consigned to the scrapheap of history but almost to disappear, leaving little but unsettling personal memories and a thin archival trace.[383]

Australian soccer is a game on the edge, literally and metaphorically. It is a foreign game and has remained so for all of the 140 years or more that Australians have been playing it. Indeed, it is sometimes a 'wicked foreign game'[384] that menaces and threatens to overrun Australian society, steal our land and brainwash and enfeeble our children. Its values and practices are 'other' and the game has periodically been asked to go back whence it came.

When it does find a temporary residence here it is often on the edge of the comfort zones of our suburbs and towns, on grounds built on industrial wastelands and recently reclaimed rubbish tips. At best the game gets to strut its stuff on borrowed, repurposed stadiums and surfaces designed and owned by and for other sports. Australian soccer has had to fight and scrap against more permanent and established residents for every piece of land to which it has access. Only rarely has such land become a settled home for the game. Freud might have described the condition of Australian soccer as *unheimlich*, in acknowledgement of its homeless and uncanny presence in Australian sports culture.

Australian soccer is a game on the edge of attention, often languishing in the shadows cast by bigger edifices, silenced by the white noise of mainstream sports trivia. Mainstream media outlets down the years have rarely supplied good coverage of the game (peak moments aside), usually relying on the nincompoopism of the circular argument: 'We don't cover it because there is little interest. Australians don't follow soccer', thereby simultaneously confessing and justifying their failure to lead or create that interest or follow whatever interest that does exist.

Since the game's codification more than 150 years ago, newspaper and other media audiences have been reminded repeatedly of how little they know about this foreign and 'brand-new' game, soccer, leaving those who consider they do know the game feeling like uninvited guests.

Soccer sits on the edge of history in Australia. It is never a core theme for the historian – though perhaps it is sometimes an interesting sideline to the main story. Historians refer habitually to its novelty, difference and foreignness. Sports histories are little better. While able to respect the game as a legitimate object of research, most are still written under the sway of the myths of soccer's marginality.

Sport historians find it harder to see soccer as a subject of research. Even those histories that profess to tell the story of the game from the inside can be diverted by the all-pervading mythologies that have built up around sport and culture in Australia. They are liable to take on board non-negotiable truths that rule the game out of the game. Some soccer historians have been complicit in their own marginalisation, happy to provide comments from the sideline rather than fight their way into the commentary box. Some of those who have made it in have found their tenure fleeting and too easily forgotten.

Australian soccer is on the edge of Australia – again in two senses. It is only played around the edges, in the big cities, home to the migrants, that leaf-fringed demense despised by the architects of bush nationalism. A D Hope's 'Australia' has this biting stanza:

> And her five cities, like five teeming sores,
> Each drains her: a vast parasite robber-state
> Where second-hand Europeans pullulate
> Timidly on the edge of alien shores.[385]

While not about soccer, Hope's poem is about its place, the 'second-hand Europeans' who live there and that place's abject relation to the spiritual centre of Australia. The rugged heart, the heroic source of real Australia is not a place of soccer.

Australian literature, legends and mythologies are constructed as soccer-free narratives and the game's intrusion in them is rare and ever dissonant when it does occur.[386] Australian soccer has no Cazaly up there with whom its players can go – whether that be to popular adulation or to their deaths in the field of battle. Unlike Australian Rules, it has no 'six-foot recruit from Eaglehawk' to provide its 'hope of salvation'.[387]

There are many Australian soccer players who have 'come down from the bush', but the game has access to no mythological narratives in which to accommodate them. The game might be able to boast Kasey Wehrman, an Aboriginal hard man from Cloncurry in north-west Queensland, but it cannot point to any archetypal bush heroes in its pantheon of greasy wogs and sneaky Scotsmen alongside whom he can sit.

Nor does Wehrman have any tangible Indigenous notables to provide fatherly mentoring. The deeds of Bondi Neal, Quilp, Charles Perkins, Gordon Briscoe, John Moriarty, Buddy Newchurch and Harry Williams could shine down the ages as beacons to young Aboriginal players because they were genuine stars of Australian soccer, a game to which Aboriginal players were sometimes welcomed in ways other codes of football found difficult.[388]

Yet these moments, like many others, have vanished from public perception and Aboriginal players are largely absent in the stories of Australian soccer. Ultimately, Australian soccer is a game on the edge of legitimacy, a game at the edge of itself. And as long as these arguments inhabit a cultural conversation that can accommodate the perversion of logic and sense that allows the nation's most played team game to be forgotten or, at best, figured as un-Australian, marginal and un-belonging, it will be ever thus.

As has been shown, the broader culture cares little for the soccer's positive memorialisation. Yet the game itself is not much better at asserting its own legitimacy or remembering its own belonging. Forgetting the game's history seems, at times, to be an imperative for soccer authorities. The transitions between significant stages of the game's history in Australia are moments in which deliberate erasure and voluntary amnesia have seemed to be vital strategies.

The rebadging of the game as soccer in the 1920s threw off the 'British' name in an attempt both to domesticate and to internationalise Association football in Australia. Even though still heavily reliant on migration from Britain, an amateur and domestically Australian-Anglo-Celtic culture emerged from the English and Scottish roots.

After the Second World War the rise to dominance of the continental European migrant clubs (and a concomitant emergence of professionalism) enabled the forgetting of that pre-war culture. For many today, soccer in Australia only really started in the 1950s. And many of the 'ethnic' clubs are guilty of 'failing' to remember their own history of supplanting a previous culture. South Melbourne Hellas is a case in point. A complex history of mergers between Australian-Anglo, Jewish and Greek clubs is lost in the club's contemporary Greek-Australian identity.

The most recent act of substantial and brutal forgetting came in 2004 with the establishment of the FFA and the A-League, led by Frank

Lowy and underpinned by the Crawford Report, which advocated substantial and important changes to the constitution and management of the game. A policy of not just forgetting but also rejecting the game's past was adopted largely because the new soccer authorities believed in the unassailability of the dominant myths that this book has tried to dismantle.

In the perceived absence of a sustained and convincing counter-narrative of soccer's legitimacy and belonging, history became a no-go zone. Indeed, the rejection of history was manifested in an advertising campaign expressing the 2006 Socceroos' intentions to play well above the level of the national team's purported historic 'mediocrity'. Even if not intended, local history was a victim of the campaign and the powerfully significant contribution of the ethnic European clubs was forgotten in the blaze of negative memories of all that was 'wrong' with 'wogball'.

When the Socceroos beat Uruguay on penalties in November 2005 they did more than fulfill a long-cherished dream of almost all Australian soccer supporters to participate again in the World Cup. The result also seemed effectively to justify, first, the decisions made about the changing of the game's ethnic identity and, second, the obliteration of the many positive things that had come from the wogball period and the 80 years before that.

Yet a review of the names of the players involved in that penalty shootout enables a profoundly beautiful realisation to emerge. Kewell, Neill, Vidmar, Viduka, Aloisi: individual players representing and embodying a progression of waves of Australian immigration: English, Irish, Slovenian, Croatian, Italian. Add the names of the crucial game-time goal-scorer, Bresciano, and the goalkeeper Schwarzer, who was responsible for two heroic shootout saves, and the multicultural diversity of Australian soccer is revealed in all its power and glory. And that is something worth remembering.

The internal denial of history is an ongoing and crippling problem for Australian soccer. The game's millions of stakeholders deserve to believe that there are reasons for optimism that the game's profound lack of self-belief and feelings of illegitimacy and unbelonging can be turned around at both national and state level. This book has revealed a deep pre-history of Australian soccer that peters out in the 1930s. It has also set the groundwork for subsequent histories.

Joe Gorman recently published *The Death and Life of Australian Soccer*, a history of Association football in Australia since the Second World War. His title deliberately inverts the natural order of individual lifecycles, referring to the death of the National Soccer League in 2004 and the birth of the A-League two years later. It is a nice metaphor and an even better narrative twist. Yet this was not the first death of Australian soccer. The game has died many times and in many places, only to be reborn and rediscovered all too often.

Perhaps soccer's first major death was in the inter-war period. Not a literal death but a spiritual one. Having survived the self-imposed hiatus and the unavoidable trauma of the First World War, soccer boomed in the early 1920s as Australians tried to regenerate their cultural lives in a time of migrant influx. The game's long, steady rise to the point where it has become Australia's major participation team sport began in the 1920s. But this rise is set against a profoundly paradoxical current: even as the game's popularity has grown, its connections to Australian myth and story have been lost. A game once firmly located in the cultures of many ordinary working-class Australians has come gradually to be seen as a foreign code that threatens the integrity and stability of Australian life.

While this is the way things are, it is not the way they have to be. Changing demographics and economics will determine shifts in Australian cultural life that are yet to take place. The future does not have to be like the past. But the great lie that soccer is the game that never happened in Australia needs to be demolished. This book intends to be a small contribution to this task.

# EPILOGUE

Soccer underwent a massive expansion in Melbourne in the late 1950s and early 1960s. Extraordinary crowds flocked to Olympic Park to watch local soccer. Over 23,000 saw a clash between George Cross and South Melbourne Hellas in 1962. In 1966 over 35,000 crammed into and around the same venue to see Victoria take on AS Roma. Simultaneously, the VFL was experiencing something of a mild decline in attendance – albeit from a relatively great height. The fear of a soccer takeover was growing once more in some VFL circles.[389] This fear sometimes turned into the active suppression of soccer through such practices as exclusion from schools, restrictive ground allocations and concerted media attacks on the game and its participants.[390]

Soccer's rise to prominence produced various responses, but perhaps none as fascinating as the idea of a soccer versus VFL match played under soccer rules. VFL media figure and ex-Richmond captain Jack Dyer challenged Slavia to a match to raise money for the Victorian Society for Crippled Children and Adults. The idea for the game came about after Dyer had been a guest of the Victorian Soccer Federation at the final of the 1964 Dockerty Cup, won by Slavia 1–0 over Footscray JUST (Jugoslav United Soccer Team). Dyer repaid his hosts' generosity by writing in his subsequent *Truth* column on 10 October, 'I went, I saw and I was sickened. Soccer . . . It really is a girls' game – but only for big girls'. He felt that if he were allowed to train the best of the VFL players in the rudiments of the game they would easily beat a team of soccer players. This rankled with a number of the Slavia team, and Dave Meechan, invited onto Channel 7's 'Wide World of Sport' by Alex Barr, suggested that Dyer should put his money where his mouth was.

The VFL players try to clear the ball against the Slavia team. Note Hammy McMeechan (in white on the right) and the incongruous 'Collingwood' banner.
Courtesy of the estate of the late Hammy McMeechan.

Dyer generated interest in the challenge by attacking the soccer players' abilities as athletes and the game itself as easy and simplistic for anyone to play. Dyer believed that VFL footballers were so physically advanced and technically skillful that playing soccer would be easy for them. Slavia accepted the challenge and the game was set for 15 November 1964. 'We've been waiting for years for this and it's here at last . . . soccer v. footy,' read one preview in the *Sporting Globe*. '"Captain Blood" [Dyer] has already warned Slavia that it's going to be "on", and this means one thing – it's going to be the toughest, roughest soccer match Victoria has ever seen'.[391]

Dyer's team included VFL luminaries Ron Barassi, Ted Whitten, Kevin Murray, Des Tuddenham and Gordon Collis. The Slavia team included Ray Barotajs, Peter Aldis, John Auchie and Hammy McMeechan – well-known in soccer circles but hardly household names in the wider Victorian community.

Some of the VFL players made their intentions clear immediately. Barassi led the charge, literally, taking every opportunity to rough-up

Slavia players. In one passage of play, Barassi charged wildly at John Auchie, who put his foot behind the ball and watched as his opponent flew through the air and landed in a crumpled, injured heap. Such was the injury that Barassi needed to leave the field. The *Age* reported that he 'had to be replaced at the interval suffering from a badly gashed leg', while the Slavia goalkeeper, Ray Barotajs, wrote for the *Truth*: 'I think the VFL boys would be the first to admit now that it isn't a girl's game – just ask Ron Barassi'.[392]

Many years later Slavia right-winger, Hammy McMeechan, met Barassi in a King Street newsagency where they happily recalled the match and the incident. McMeechan claimed that Barassi told him, 'That was the injury that eventually made me give footy away'.[393]

In another passage of play, McMeechan ran on to a through ball with his marker, Gordon Collis, in tow. He could feel Collis's massive frame bearing down on him and so did a neat backheel to his captain and right-half, John Sanchez. Instead of stopping, McMeechan kept racing toward the corner flag with Collis still in hot pursuit. Arriving at the flag McMeechan turned around with his arms outstretched as if to say to Collis, 'What are you going to do now?' Collis turned away seething, to the amusement of the massive crowd.

'It was a little spiteful in that we, with our technique, couldn't resist the opportunity of a hip and shoulder here and there,' Collis told the *Age* in 2009. 'The other boys had tricks of their own. One of them was to put a foot over the ball as you were about to kick it, so your shins would make contact with the soles of their boots. That didn't improve relations. We didn't see it as very manly way of going about things. But it was effective. It was also effective in stirring us up!'

At half time the score was 3–0 to Slavia, comfortable without being comprehensive. Having by now recognised what was an obvious mismatch, some representatives of the VFL players came into the Slavia dressing room asking if they could play Australian Rules in the second half. The Slavia coach, former Manchester United player Brian Birch, said 'Look at my players. Hammy's the biggest forward and he's only 5' 6". No way. We never said we could beat you at your game!'

In the end Slavia won 8–0 in a game that lasted less than an hour, as opposed to the regulation 90 minutes. In what must have been something of a culture shock a few things were revealed to the sporting public well beyond the players who participated. First, the might of the VFL had been beaten by a team of part-timers, none of whom would rank in the top thousand players in the world. Second, soccer was shown to have its own requirements of strength and fitness. While few would ignore the sheer toughness and durability required to play Australian Rules football, too many are prepared to downplay the physical demands of soccer. While John Auchie's tackle had an unfortunate impact, it nonetheless demonstrated the different kind of balance of technique, strength and toughness required to play the round-ball game.

But the most important lesson was that for too long many Australians had failed and perhaps still fail to understand the technical skill and artistry of the world game and the physical qualities needed to play even at a moderate semi-professional level.

In a different space or time this might have been the kind of event that changed the way a culture behaved. Indeed, even Jack Dyer begrudgingly accepted defeat and agreed that he was surprised by the skills of the soccer players.[394] The moment was right for a Victorian accord based on the mutual respect developed between the players and shared by the majority of the spectators on the day. The moment was also right for soccer to come into mainstream culture as a legitimate sports option for Australian children and adults. The game could lose its mysterious foreign shadow and cease to be mocked and ridiculed by professional media boofheads like Dyer and the gullible among their readers, viewers and listeners.

It was not to be. Within months Dyer was back to his baiting best – though he never made the mistake of challenging the 'soccer boys' again. The lessons were forgotten and normal service was resumed. 'Wogball' was consigned once more to the margins of Australian life where it quietly got on with the never-ending business of tearing itself apart and rebuilding and tearing itself apart and – remaining, indeed, the game that never happened.

# REFERENCES

Abrams, Lynn. *Oral History Theory*. London: Routledge, 2016.

Alomes, Stephen. *Australian Football: The People's Game 1958–2058*. Petersham, NSW: Walla Walla Press, 2012.

Andrews, E.M. *The Anzac Illusion*. Cambridge: Cambridge University Press, 1993.

Bailey, Stephen. 'Living Sports History: Football at Winchester, Eton and Harrow'. *The Sports Historian*. 15 May 1995, 2–3.

Barker, Anthony J. *Behind the Play: A History of Football in Western Australia from 1868*, Perth: Western Australian Football Commission, 2004.

Bean, CEW. *Official History of Australia in the War of 1914–1918. Volume I: The Story of ANZAC from the outbreak of war to the end of the first phase of the Gallipoli Campaign, May 4, 1915* (11th edition, 1941) https://www.awm.gov.au/collection/C1416845 (accessed 16/4/2018).

Blackburn, Kevin. *War, Sport and the ANZAC Tradition*. London: Palgrave, 2016.

Blainey, Geoffrey. *A Game of Our Own: The Origins of Australian Rules Football*. Melbourne: Information Australia, 1990.

Blair, Dale. 'Beyond the metaphor: football and war, 1914–1918'. *Journal of the Australian War Memorial*. 28, April 1996 https://www.awm.gov.au/articles/journal/j28/j28-blai (accessed 16/4/2018).

Booth, Douglas and Colin Tatz. *One-Eyed: A View of Australian Sport*. St Leonards, NSW, Allen and Unwin, 2000.

Cashman, Richard. *Sport in the National Imagination: Australian Sport in the Federation Decades*. Sydney: Walla Walla Press, 2002.

Cazaly, Ciannon. 'Off the Ball: Football's History Wars'. *Meanjin*. 67:4, Summer 2008, 82–7.

Collins, Tony, 'The Invention of Sporting Tradition: National Myths, Imperial Pasts and the Origins of Australian Rules Football'. In Stephen Wagg (ed.). *Myths and Milestones in the History of Sport*, 8–31. London: Palgrave Macmillan, 2011.

Dawe, Bruce. 'Life–cycle', Sometimes Gladness: *Collected Poems, 1954–1982*. Melbourne: Longman, 1983.

Dunning, Eric and Kenneth Sheard. *Barbarians, Gentlemen and Players.* Canberra: Australian National University Press, 1979.

Fiddian, Marc. *Forever Fitzroy: A History of the Brunswick St Oval.* Hastings, Vic.: Galaxy Print and Design, c2004.

Fink, Jesse. 'The FFA's Denying of History'. *The World Game.* 4 January 2010. http://theworldgame.sbs.com.au/jesse fink/blog/408210/The-FFA-s-denying-of-history (accessed 8/1/2018).

Fortier, Anne-Marie. *Migrant Belongings.* Oxford: Berg, 2000.

Fujak, Hunter and Stephen Frawley. 'The Barassi Line: Quantifying Australia's Great Sporting Divide'. *Sporting Traditions.* 30:2, November 2013, 93–109.

Gorman, Joe. *The Death and Life of Australian Soccer.* Brisbane: University of Queensland Press, 2017.

Gorman, Sean. *Legends: The AFL Indigenous Team of the Century.* Canberra: Aboriginal Studies Press, 2011.

Grant, Sidney James. *Jack Pollard's Soccer Records.* Sydney: Jack Pollard, n.d. [1974].

Green, Jonathan. 'Anzac Day is about their deaths, not our lives'. *The Drum.* 25 April 2012. www.abc.net.au/news/2012-04-25/green-anzac-day-lest-we-forget/3971574 (accessed 8/1/2018).

Hajkowicz Stefan, Hannah Cook, Lisa Wilhelmseder and Naomi Broughen. *Future of Australian Sport: Megatrends shaping the sprots sector over the coming decades. A Consultancy Report for the Australian Sports Commission.* Canberra: CSIRO, 2013.

Hay, Roy. 'British Football, Wogball or the World Game? Towards a Social History of Victorian Soccer'. In John O'Hara (ed.). Ethnicity and Soccer in Australia, 44–79. *ASSH Studies in Sports History* 10. Campbelltown, NSW: Australian Society for Sports History, 1994.

Hay, Roy. 'Football's First Free Kick: Demography and the Media – How and Why Australia Got a Game of Its Own'. *The International Journal of the History of Sport.* 33:3, 2016, 289–305.

Hay, Roy. 'Football in Australia before Codification, 1820–1860'. *The International Journal of the History of Sport.* 31:9, 2014, 1047–61.

Hay, Roy. 'Henry John Dockerty, 1882–1965'. *Neos Osmos.* 15 May 2012. http://neososmos.blogspot.com.au/2012/05/henry-john-dockerty-18821965.html (accessed 8/1/2018).

Hay, Roy. '"Our Wicked Foreign Game": Why has Association football (soccer) not become the main code of football in Australia?' *Soccer and Society.* 7:2–3, 2006, 165–86.

Hay, Roy. Review of Matthew J McDowell, *A Cultural History of Association Football in Scotland 1865–1902.* Lampeter, Wales: Edwin Mellen Press, 2013.

Hay, Roy and Bill Murray. *A History of Football in Australia*, Melbourne, Hardie Grant, 2014.

Hay, Roy and Ian Syson. *The Story of Football in Victoria.* Melbourne: Football Federation Victoria, 2009.

Hess, Rob, Matthew Nicholson, Bob Stewart and Gregory de Moore. *A National Game: The History of Australian Rules Football*. Melbourne: Penguin, 2008.

Hibbins, GM. 'The Cambridge Connection: The Origin of Australian Rules Football'. *The International Journal of the History of Sport*. 6:2, 1989, 172–92.

Hibbins, Gillian. 'Myth and History in Australian Rules Football'. *Sporting Traditions*. 25:2, November 2008, 41–53.

Hobsbawm, Eric and Terence Ranger (eds). *The Invention of Tradition*. Cambridge: Cambridge University Press, 1983.

Hope, A D. 'Australia'. In H Hesletine (ed.). *The Penguin Book of Australian Verse*. Ringwood, Vic.: Penguin, 1972.

Hudson, Chris. *A Century of Soccer, 1898-1998: A Tasmanian History*. Hobart: Peacock, 1998.

Kallinikios, John. *Soccer Boom: The Transformation of Victorian Soccer Culture, 1945–1963*. Sydney: Walla Walla Press, 2007.

Kitching, Gavin. ' "Old" Football and the "New" Codes: Some Thoughts on the "Origins of Football" Debate and Suggestions for Further Research'. *The International Journal of the History of Sport*. 28:13, September 2011, 1733–49.

Kreider, Richard. *The Soccerites*. Perth: SportsWest Media, 2005.

Lake, Marilyn, Henry Reynolds and Mark McKenna. *What's Wrong With Anzac? The Militarisation of Australian History*. Sydney: University of New South Wales Press, 2010.

Mangan, Patrick. *Offsider*. Melbourne: Victory, 2010.

Markovits, Andrei S and Lars Rensmann. *Gaming the World: How Sports are Reshaping Global Politics and Culture*. New Jersey: Princeton Univesisty Press, 2010.

Mavroudis, Paul. 'Against the Run of Play: The Emergence of Australian Soccer Literature'. *The International Journal of the History of Sport*. 30:5, 2013, 484–99.

Maynard, John. *The Aboriginal Soccer Tribe: A History of Aboriginal Involvement with the World Game*. Broome: Magabala, 2011.

McKenna, Peter. *My World of Football*. North Sydney, NSW: Pollard Publishing, 1973.

Melbourne Cricket Ground Trust. 'Soccer'. http://www.mcg.org.au/the-stadium/mcg-history/soccer (accessed 8/1/2018).

Mosely, Philip. 'Soccer'. In Wray Vamplew et al. (eds). *The Oxford Companion to Australian Sport*. 385–88. Melbourne: Oxford University Press, 1998.

Mosely, Philip. *Soccer in New South Wales, 1880–1980*. Bannockburn and Carlton North, Vic.: Sports and Editorial Services Australia in association with Vulgar Press, 2014.

Mosely, Philip and Bill Murray. 'Soccer'. In Wray Vamplew and Brian Stoddardt (eds). *Sport in Australia: A Social History*, 213–30. Cambridge: Cambridge University Press, 1994.

Murphy, Brendan. *From Sheffield With Love*. York, UK: SportsBooks, 2007.

Murray, David. *Memories of the Old College of Glasgow: Some Chapters in the History of the University*, Glasgow: Jackson, Wylie, 1927.

Nicolussi, Christian. 'Preston the pocket rocket'. *Daily Telegraph*, 30 May 2008. www.dailytelegraph.com.au/sport/nrl/preston-the-pocket-rocket/story-e6frexsi-1111116481103 (accessed 8/1/2018).

Pearson, Harry. *The Far Corner: A Mazy Dribble through North-East Football*. London: Little, Brown, 1994.

Phillips, Murray G. 'Sport, War and Gender Images: The Australian Sportsmen's Battalions and the First World War'. *The International Journal of the History of Sport*. 14:1, 1997, 78–96.

Pinchin, Ken. *A Century of Tasmanian Football, 1879–1979*. Launceston: Tasmanian Football League, 1979.

Power, Thomas P. *The Footballer: An Annual RECORD of Football in Victoria, 1875*. Melbourne: Henriques, 1875.

Queensland Health – Mental Health. 'The road to recovery – a history of mental health services in Queensland 1859-2009'. www.health.qld.gov.au/mentalhealth/docs/qld-mh-history.pdf (accessed 3/12/2012).

Reeves, Andrew. *Up from the Underworld: Coalminers and Community in Wonthaggi 1909–1968*. Melbourne: Monash University Press, 2011.

Roberts, Phil. *Roosters: The History of the North Ballarat Football Club*. Ballarat: North Ballarat Football Club, 2003.

Sandercock, Leonie and Ian Turner. *Up Where, Cazaly? The Great Australian Game*. Sydney: Granada, 1982.

Sanders, Richard. *Beastly Fury*. Harmondsworth: Penguin, 2010.

Stråth, Bo. 'Belonging and European Identity'. in Gerard Delanty, Ruth Wodak and Paul Jones (eds). *Identity, Belonging and Migration*, 21–37. Liverpool: Liverpool University Press, 2007.

Suchman, Mark C. 'Managing Legitimacy: Strategic and Institutional Approaches'. *Academy of Management Journal*. 20:3, 1995, 571–610.

Tasmania AFL: It's Time. 'A History of Football in Tasmania'. http://www.tassiefootyteam.com.au/history.php (accessed 3/12/2012).

Thompson, David. *The Rules That Made Australian Football*. Sydney: Walla Walla Press, 2013.

Thompson, E P. *The Making of the English Working Class*. Harmondsworth: Penguin, 1980.

Thompson, Trevor. *One Fantastic Goal: A Complete History of Football in Australia*. Sydney: ABC Books, 2006.

University of Glasgow. 'The University of Glasgow Story'. http://universitystory.gla.ac.uk/biography/?id=WH12325&type=P (accessed 8/1/2018).

Warren, John with Andy Harper and Josh Whittington. *Sheilas, Wogs and Poofters: An Incomplete Biography of Johnny Warren and Soccer in Australia*. Sydney: Random, 2002.

Warrnambool Football Netball Club. 'History of Warrnambool FC'. Sporting Pulse. www.sportingpulse.com/club_info.cgi?c=1-6167-80605-0-11780475&sID=217328 (accessed 8/1/2018).

Weston, James (ed.). *The Australian Game of Football Since 1858*. Melbourne: Geoff Slattery Publishing, 2008.

Williams, Raymond. *Marxism and Literature*. Oxford: Oxford University Press, 1977.

Williamson, John. *Soccer Anzacs: The Story of Caledonian Soccer Club*. Applecross, WA, John Williamson, 1998.

Young, David. *Sporting Island: A History of Sport and Recreation in Tasmania*. Hobart: Department of Sport and Recreation Tasmania, 2005.

# NOTES

1    Suchman adopts this definition of legitimacy: 'a generalized perception or assumption that the actions of an entity are desirable, proper, or appropriate within some socially constructed system of norms, values, beliefs, and definitions', 'Managing Legitimacy', 574. It uses ideas of constructed social norms against which actions and behaviours are measured.

2    Stråth provides a definition of belonging as it applies to Europe: 'belonging stands for social inclusion under conditions of cultural diversity', 'Belonging and European Identity', 36. This is a useful definition of belonging as I intend to use it in this book.

3    Fortier, *Migrant Belongings*, 2.

4    The 'Barassi Line' is an imaginary line drawn across Australia that divides the country culturally into Australian Rules and Rugby zones. See Fujak and Frawley, 'The Barassi Line,' 94.

5    Much of the research for this book has been conducted within the online digital newspaper facility provided by Trove at the National Library of Australia. The history presented one of a new post-digitisation kind, which, given the widespread availability of searchable and digitised newspaper archives, is more easily able to identify and capture archival material than in previous times. This capacity is both a strength and a weakness of such research. The technology facilitates and promotes the quotation and assimilation of a great volume of primary text into the body of the book. This is advantageous to my interests because it enhances the texturing of the book using the language of the period in question. It enables the easy representation of both the content and the form of the material being cited. Given that the rhetoric of inclusion and exclusion is one of my central themes, this new-found efficiency of capture is a boon.

6    Abrams, *Oral History Theory*, 97.

7    'Participation in outdoor soccer has experienced significant growth between 2001 and 2010, from 551,300 participants (Dale and Ford, 2001) to 843,900 (Standing Committee on Recreation and Sport, 2010)' (Hajkowicz, Cook, Wilhelmseder and Boughen, *Future of Australian Sport*, 23). The Australian game's peak body, FFA, claimed in 2013 that nearly 1 million people were registered participants while 2 million people in total participated in the game as players, officials or coaches at formal and informal levels ('Football participation reaches 1.96 million Australians', 12 November 2013. http://www.footballaustralia.com.au/news-display/article/Football-participation-reaches-1.96-million-Australians/78074. http://www.ausport.gov.au/__data/assets/pdf_file/0007/653875/34648_AusPlay_summary_report_accessible_FINAL_updated_211216.pdf.

8    A key difference today might be that children *are* beginning to support both soccer and the 'other' code, whatever that may be.

9    McKenna, *My World of Football*, 9; Gorman, *Legends*, 156.

10   Nicolussi, 'Preston the pocket rocket'. This observation applies not just to football codes. The test-cricketing Waugh brothers both had to make a decision whether to leave soccer for professional cricket in the mid-to-late-teens. Young Australian soccer player Christian Vieri was lost to *Australian* soccer when he went straight to Italy.

11  The best coverage of these issues is in the vast body of work by Roy Hay. See especially Hay, ' "Our Wicked Foreign Game" '.

12  Warren et al., *Sheilas, Wogs and Poofters*, xxi–xxii.

13  Flanagan, 'The meaning of football', *Age*, 10 February 2004.

14  Duffy, 'Jig is up – give World Cup the boot'. *Sydney Morning Herald*, 2 September 2006.

15  Sanderson, 'Bend It Like (Yogi) Berra'. *Library of Economics and Liberty*, 7 August 2006.

16  Duffy, 'Jig is up – give World Cup the boot'. *Sydney Morning Herald*, 2 September 2006.

17  Dunning and Sheard, *Barbarians, Gentlemen and Players*, 23.

18  Markovits and Rensmann, *Gaming the World*, 76.

19  Flanagan, 'Footy should stand by its history'. *Age*, 10 December 2005.

20  Alomes, *Australian Football*, 127.

21  Interestingly, if the Victorian Football Association (VFA) had been wiped out by the Victorian Football League (VFL) (in line with some Australian Rules visions), 'Association' would have been a dormant term and available for soccer's use. One possible result could have been the organisational names, Association football (soccer) and League football (Australian Rules) in Victoria.

22  Thompson, *The Rules that Made Australian Football*.

23  This is acknowledged in the title of Hess et al., *A National Game: The History of Australian Rules Football*, possibly the most comprehensive history of Australian Rules yet published.

24  *Maitland Mercury and Hunter River General Advertiser* 26 April 1883, 7; 19 July 1883, 4.

25  *Australian Town and Country Journal*, 21 July 1894, 39

26  Thompson, *The Making of the English Working Class*, 9.

27  The *Sydney Monitor* reported on 27 July 1829, 4: 'The privates in the barracks are in the habit of amusing themselves with the game of foot-ball; the ball may be daily descried repeatedly mounting higher or lower, according to the skill and energy of the bold military kickers thereof. It is a healthy amusement, and much played in Leicestershire.'

There are extensive metaphoric uses of the term football in the early Australian press suggesting that the awareness (if not necessarily the practice) of football was common among early white Australians. The earliest I have found was in the *Sydney Gazette and New South Wales Advertiser*, 24 August 1816, 2. Davenports in Sydney advertised footballs for sale in the *Sydney Herald*, 19 June 1837, 3.

28  Hay, 'Football in Australia before Codification', 1048.

29  As late as 1888, the secretary of the Victorian Football Association was arguing for the introduction of a rugby-type crossbar (*Argus*, 12 April 1888, 8).

30  *Brisbane Courier*, 11 June 1866, 3; *Queenslander*, 16 June 1866, 12.

31  *Queenslander*, 4 July 1868, 9.

32  *Bell's Life in Sydney and Sporting Chronicle*, 21 August 1869, 3.

33  *Bell's Life in Sydney and Sporting Chronicle*, 28 August 1869, 3.

34  *Bell's Life in Sydney and Sporting Chronicle*, 18 June 1870, 4.

35  *Register*, 1 July 1907, 5.

36  Hay, 'Football in Australia before Codification', 1054.

37  Bailey, 'Living Sports History', 2–3.

38  'Harrow Football'. http://www.youtube.com/watch?v=4qDzSmDqcTQ (accessed 10/2/2016). It is not difficult to see a direct lineage from a game like Harrow football to both Australian Rules and soccer. Removing the offside law and adding running with the ball (with periodic bouncing) and tackling to the Harrow game would result in a game very similar to contemporary Australian Rules. Preventing handling, modifying the offside rule and adding a crossbar would produce something akin to soccer.

39  *South Australian Register*, 14 May 1873, 5.

40  *Argus*, 10 August 1874, 1S.

41  *South Australian Advertiser*, 22 July 1876, 4.

42  *South Australian Advertiser*, 12 August 1876, 4.

43  *South Australian Advertiser*, 5 June 1878, 3.

44  See Chapter 2.

45   *Bell's Life in Sydney and Sporting Chronicle*, 27 July 27 1867, 3.

46   *Bell's Life in Sydney and Sporting Chronicle*, 17 August 1867, 3.

47   *Bell's Life in Sydney and Sporting Chronicle*, 21 August 1869, 3. The manual mentioned is *Mahon's Cricket and Sports Manual: comprising cricket, rounders, football, bowls, quoits, and athletic sports: with hints on training, & c.*, edited by Mr. PC Curtis (Sydney, McMahon, 1869).

48   *Australian Town and Country Journal*, 21 May 1870, 27.

49   *Brisbane Courier*, 3 May 1876, 3.

50   It also adopted a new name, the Bonnet Rouge Football Club. See Chapter 2.

51   *Brisbane Courier*, 17 June 1876, 5. The article also appeared in the Hobart *Mercury*, 6 July 1876, 3.

52   *Australasian,* 29 May 1869, 12.

53   *Argus, 23* September 1873, 7.

54   A pen name of John Walter Fletcher, according to Mosely, *Soccer in New South Wales, 1880–1980*, 11.

55   *Argus*, 28 April 1874, 6; *Portland Guardian and Normanby General Advertiser* also published the rules (reprinted from the *Australasian*) three days later but without any accompanying text (1 May 1874, 2). 'C.C.' also wrote a letter advocating soccer to the *Sydney Morning Herald* on 15 May 1877, 5. 'Old Rugbeian' responded on 23 May 1877, 6.

56   *Argus*, 11 August 1879, 7.

57   *Argus*, 13 August 1879, 7.

58   *Sydney Morning Herald*, 31 August 1878, 7. This may yet bear out to be an error. The game might have been Victorian Rules and Rugby. The newspaper confused matters in its earlier report: 'The contest was arranged, primarily, with the object of giving that section of the public who take an interest in this winter pastime an opportunity of contrasting the Victorian, or more properly speaking, English Association game, with the Rugby' (26 August 1878, 6).

59   Hay, 'Football's First Free Kick'.

60   Hay, 'Football's First Free Kick', 299.

61   The very first game in Hobart was played without goalposts. Coats were used to mark the goals. See Chapter 2.

62   See *Sydney Herald*, 19 June 1837, 3; *Colonist*, 19 December 1838, 3.

63   *Sydney Morning Herald*, 12 February 1866, 6

64   *Launceston Examiner*, 26 February 1865, 5.

65   *Argus*, 6 June 1862, 3.

66   *Argus*, 17 June 1864, 8.

67   *Mercury*, 22 April, 1873, 3.

68   *Mercury*, 4 April 1879, 2

69   *Launceston Examiner*, 17 November 1860, 4.

70   Power, *The Footballer*, 5.

71   *Argus*, 11 September 1865, 5.

72   Hess et al. *A National Game*, 36.

73   *South Australian Advertiser*, 12 August 1876, 4.

74   *Mercury*, April 4, 1879, 2.

75   This notion is from Hibbins, 'The Cambridge Connection', 180.

76   Young, *Sporting Island*, 143.

77   Mangan's *Offsider* gives us a humorous and more contemporary look at the problem of a soccerista's marginality in rural Victoria.

78   Though Hibbins makes it clear that 'kicking-only (incipient soccer) proponents' were thereabouts at the formation Melbourne Rules, implying that early Melbourne Rules embodied a soccerite impulse. She writes that the 'problem for the "kickers-only" was that, although they had the numbers at meetings [. . .] the silent majority it would seem were already playing, and inclined towards Rugby School-style football' (Hibbins, 1989, 180). This notion of soccer dominating the numbers at meetings while not representing the popular view is applicable to early football development and codification across a number of Australian cities.

79   *Argus*, 9 July 1870, 4.

80    The *Australasian* used the more definitive 'rules' rather than 'style': 'In order to make the game as equal as possibly both teams will play according to the "home rules", which provide that there shall be no holding or running with the ball' (9 July 1870, 11).

81    *Argus*, 11 July 1870, 5.

82    The point might also be made that the game bears little resemblance to the written Melbourne Rules of the time and virtually no likeness to Australian Rules as played today. Then again the Melbourne Rules of the time bear little resemblance to Australian Rules of today either, which begs the question of when Australian Rules football actually began. The myth says 1858/1859. The principles that form the basis of a code – for this author, established and relatively stable rules agreed and conformed to by an associated community of clubs – says 1877, at the earliest.

83    Mosely covers this moment in some depth. He points out that five correspondents urged the formation of a soccer body at this time (Moseley, *Soccer in New South Wales*, 9). Thompson believes that it was a coordinated campaign. He describes it as a 'wave of letters' (Thompson, *One Fantastic Goal*, 21).

84    The reference to the Victorian Association game is to the game of football administered by the Victorian Football Association (VFA) of the time.

85    *Sydney Morning Herald*, 17 July 1880, 6.

86    Hibbins, 'Myth and History in Australian Rules Football,' 6.

87    Given the superficial similarities observed or assumed by many at the time, Fletcher is either seeing the differences in socio-political terms or is focusing on the absence of offside in the Victorian game. To the point about offside, in 1880 Fletcher represents a public-school strain within soccer that will soon wither to residual status. The eventual offside law is an accommodation between the hard and fast public-school offside laws and the Sheffield Rules' absence of offside. Interestingly it is a habit of mind among Australian Rules aficionados to see equivalence between soccer and rugby's offside rules. Soccer's contemporary offside rule is actually quite liberal compared with rugby and the relative freedom to move in soccer (the fact that it is usually perfectly legal to receive the ball when in front of the kicker) makes it closer to the liberties of Australian Rules than the hard offside line in both rugby codes.

88    *Sydney Morning Herald*, 3 August 1880, 6.

89    *Sydney Morning Herald*, 18 August 1880, 6.

90    *Sydney Morning Herald*, 24 August 1880, 6.

91    *Australian Town and Country Journal*, 28 August 1880, 35.

92    *Mercury*, 28 April 1879, 2.

93    *Mercury*, 4 May 1878, 2.

94    At this meeting the knowledge of standing orders seemed as important as the desire of its members. Launceston's *Cornwall Chronicle* suggested that Boddam or others corrupted the process by inviting non-members to vote (7 May 1879, 2).

95    *Tasmanian Mail*, 10 May 1879, 19.

96    *Mercury*, 12 May 1879, 3.

97    *Mercury*, 12 May 1879, 3.

98    *Mercury*, 9 June 1879, 2.

99    *Tasmanian Mail*, 14 June 1879, 19.

100   *Mercury*, 13 May 1879, 2.

101   *Mercury*, 3 May 1877, 2.

102   *Tasmanian Mail*, 1 September 1877, 19.

103   *Tasmanian Mail*, 29 June 1878, 19.

104   *Mercury*, 17 December 1878, 1S.

105   *Mercury*, 22 September 1931, 9.

106   *Mercury*, 15 September 1936, 11.

107   *Mercury*, 6 July 1881, 3.

108   *Mercury*, 11 July 1881, 2.

109   *Launceston Examiner*, 27 June 1887, 3.

110   Hess et al., *A National Game*, 97–8.

111   *Mercury*, 16 June 1879, 2.

112 *Mercury*, 31 May 1883, 2.

113 *Mercury*, 13 May 1884, 3.

114 This is a phrase often used to describe Australian Rules football *vis-à-vis* 'foreign' codes. Cf. Blainey, *A Game of Our Own*.

115 *Mercury*, 29 September 1879, 3.

116 See Chapter 1.

117 Fink, 'The FFA's Denying of History.'

118 Tasmania AFL: It's Time, 'A History of Football in Tasmania'. Pinchin's history of Tasmanian football, *A Century of Tasmanian Football*, makes a similar elision. It notes the turmoil and debate surrounding the ascendancy of Melbourne Rules in 1879 without registering the competing interest from other codes of football (see 11, 23, 25).

119 Blainey, *A Game of Our Own*, 80.

120 Young, *Sporting Island*, 110.

121 Young, *Sporting Island*, 62.

122 Eric Hobsbawm has shown the folly in the invention of tradition in this manner (Hobsbawm and Ranger, *The Invention of Tradition*). The AFL is, understandably, the main mythologiser of the origins of Australian Rules football. In 2008 it celebrated the purported 150th anniversary of the game and lent its support to the publication of James Weston's *The Australian Game of Football Since 1858*, a landmark book that engages in the colonisation of the past.

123 An example of this can be found in Phil Roberts' history of the North Ballarat Roosters. Citing an example of an 11-a-side game in Melbourne in 1850, Roberts suggests that whether 'this was an "Aussie Rules" game is open to question, but it is evidence of the start of Melbourne's football' (Roberts, *Roosters*, 2003) It is simply not open to question because it could *not* have been Australian Rules. But the rhetorical trick has already been taken. Merely raising the question introduces the notion that even if it is not Australian Rules *per se*, because it occurred in the city that came to be dominated by Australian Rules it is therefore Australian Rules *in embryo*.

 Evidence suggests that Warrnambool Football club was established as an 'English Football' club in 1861. According to the club's website, it was established on 4 June 1861. Warrnambool was the scene of a game of 'English football' in which two goals were scored. Shortly after the second of them the ball burst, bringing a premature end to the proceedings, with no victor declared. However, the sport itself appears to have been a winner, and today's Warrnambool Football Club traces its origins all the way back to that winter of 1861, making it among the oldest football clubs in Australia.

 Warrnambool is a town on Victoria's western coast. In the 1860s it was an isolated settlement mainly accessed by sea.

 Collins, in his 'The Invention of Sporting Tradition', conducts an extensive and devastating deconstruction of Australian Rules football's origin myths. These myths are also discussed by Gillian Hibbins, 'Myth and History in Australian Rules Football'.

124 Hess et al., *A National Game*, 3.

125 Hay, 'Football in Australia Before Codification'.

126 Hudson, *A Century of Soccer*, 9.

127 This criticism is made from a post-digitisation standpoint in which access to digital newspaper archives has enabled researchers to avoid much of the archival slog required in the past. Hudson was unable to perform the kind of term searches that have enabled this criticism.

128 *Mercury*, 3 July 1926, 5.

129 *Mercury*, 8 August 1876, 3.

130 *Queenslander*, 14 August 1875, 6; *Brisbane Courier*, 9 August 1875, 3.

131 Power, *The Footballer*, 80.

132 Power, *The Footballer*, 80. The other games are described as Rugby Union.

133 This is a matter for conjecture and further research, but the choice may also have been determined by assumptions about what would or would not be an appropriate game for inmates to play.

134 *Brisbane Courier*, 14 September 1877, 3; University of Glasgow, 'The University of Glasgow

Story'; *Brisbane Courier*, 14 June 1869, 2; *Warwick Examiner and Times*, 3 June 1871, 2.

135 Queensland Health – Mental Health, 'The road to recovery – a history of mental health services in Queensland 1859–2009'.

136 *Brisbane Courier*, 17 November 1873, 3.

137 Murray, *Memories of The Old College of Glasgow*, 444.

138 Quoted in Kitching, ' "Old" Football and the "New" Codes', 1748.

139 There are many mentions of local Association rules in the Rockhampton press in the early 1880s. It is unclear whether these refer to soccer or Victorian Rules.

140 *Sydney Morning Herald*, 26 August 1878, 6.

141 *The Australasian Sketcher with Pen and Pencil* felt the game was adaptable for all who came. Its rules 'are very simple, and such as a player fresh from Rugby, Winchester, or Eton, or, in fact, anywhere, can easily accommodate himself to after a very short acquaintance' (12 June 1875, 39). The *Sketcher* misunderstands the desire for and felt necessity of offside in the ball-handling games.

142 Reviewing Matthew McDowell's book on football in the west of Scotland at the turn of the twentieth century, Roy Hay noted: 'The role of the press in relation to the emerging sports, particularly football, is carefully examined, though the author may have misinterpreted a reference to two association football matches in Melbourne which according to the *Scottish Umpire* attracted 10,000 spectators in 1884. These were most likely games under the auspices of the Victorian Football Association, playing the Australian game. The inter-colonial soccer matches the previous year attracted around 200 and club matches in 1884 were very much participant rather than spectator games'. See also 'Football in Australia', *Dundee Courier & Argus*, 26 January 1882.

143 Free kick, 'Football in Melbourne', letter to *Bell's Life in Victoria*, 14 May 1864, 2. 'Free kick' is mistakenly assumed to be Wills by Sandercock and Turner, *Up Where Cazaly?*, 28.

144 Murphy, *From Sheffield With Love*, 40–1.

145 'Free Kick', 'Football in Melbourne', letter to *Bell's Life in Victoria*, 14 May 1864, 2.

146 Sandercock and Turner, *Up Where Cazaly?*, 27.

147 Tony Collins takes Ciannon Cazaly 'Off the Ball' to task on her own anachronistic insertion of contemporary Australian Rules into the Melbourne Rules of the 1860s. She quoted James Dawson's 1881 account of the ball being kicked high in an Aboriginal game and concluded by saying 'to me, that sounds a lot like what happens at the MCG most weekends . . .' The problem, of course, is that this is an anachronism – the description may sound like what happens at the MCG *today*, but it does not sound like an Australian Rules match during the sport's formative period.

   Indeed, the now characteristic 'high mark' of current-day Australian Rules, where a player leaps above an opponent to catch the ball in the air, seems only to begin to become a significant feature of the game in the mid-1870s, almost 20 years after the first rules were drawn up. In its 1876 edition the handbook of the game, the *Footballer*, advised players to avoid 'jumping for marks' because of its danger. Rugby-style loose scrummaging was a more important part of the game in its early years than the high mark (see Collins, 'The Invention of Sporting Tradition').

148 Collins, 'The Invention of Sporting Tradition', 16.

149 Hess et al. point out that 'the early descriptions of the game played under Melbourne Rules – at least for the first two decades after its creation … make it clear that it was characterised by play that was close to the ground. The play involved repeated scrimmages and the emphasis was on a bulk of players to move the ball forward. There are no references to high marking as a characteristic on any kind of regular basis that would suggest it was a key part of the early game' (Hess et al., *A National Game*, 56).

150 *Melbourne Punch*, 30 September 1858, 7.

151 http://www.boylesfootballphotos.net.au/article42-Football-in-the-Illustrated-Newspapers-1860-1890 (accessed 16/5/18).

152 *Footballer* 1879, 13.

153 An illustration in Sanders, *Beastly Fury* (84–5) suggests that the piece was first published in *Beaton's Annual* 1866.

154 *Argus*, 6 April 1883, 3.
155 *Australasian Sketcher with Pen and Pencil*, 7 May 1883. It might be churlish to make the point that soccer has outlasted the journal (which closed its doors in 1889).
156 *Argus*, 17 August 1883, 7.
157 *Age*, 17 August 1883.
158 *Argus*, 20 August 1883, 10.
159 *Argus*, 17 August 1883, 7.
160 See also Hay, 'British Football, Wogball or the World Game', 47. Hay draws the inference wryly: 'Soccer players are not only degenerate but sneaky. They would not involve themselves in the manly violence of Australian Rules, but resorted instead to surreptitious and underhand mayhem'. This idea is repeated by Collis in his memory of the Slavia game (see the Epilogue).
161 *Argus*, 27 August 1883, 9.
162 *South Australian Register*, 25 August 1883, 6.
163 Indeed, 30 years later in far away Coraki in northern NSW, in a different state with a different hegemonic code of football, the first response to soccer is nearly identical, as if it were constructed from the same template: 'The first game of football played at Coraki under British Association rules took place on Saturday, when Oakland defeated Coraki rather easily. Included in the winning team were several "soccer" cracks, who put up an attractive game, but otherwise the match was not as interesting as those witnessed under Rugby Union rules. Even allowing that Saturday's teams were comprised largely of novices, it does not seem,' writes the *Star*'s Coraki correspondent, 'that the popularity of the Rugby game is likely to be endangered' (*Northern Star*, 11 July 1911, 5).
164 Collins, 'The Invention of Sporting Tradition', 21.
165 Collins, 'The Invention of Sporting Tradition', 21.
166 *Argus*, 19 August 1884, 7.
167 *Gippsland Times*, 7 July 1884, 3.
168 *Argus*, 16 April 1885, 10.
169 *Argus*, 23 March 1885, 10.
170 *Argus*, 20 July 1883, 7. An article reporting on this game and explaining soccer rules appeared in the *Launceston Examiner* on 25 July 1885, S1.
171 *Argus*, 11 May 1886, 9; 14 June 1886, 5.
172 *Argus*, 25 May 1886, 5.
173 *Argus*, 3 May 1887, 10.
174 While this is probably the first time organised 11-a-side soccer was played at the venue, the Caledonian soccer small-sided soccer tournament was held there earlier (*Argus*, 17 March 1886, 6).
175 Melbourne Cricket Ground Trust, 'Soccer.'
176 *Portland Guardian*, 14 May 1888, 3.
177 *South Australian Register*, 11 June 1888, 5.
178 *South Australian Register*, 20 August 1888, 5.
179 *Argus*, 2 July 1888, 5.
180 *Argus*, 5 July 1888, 5.
181 *Argus*, 30 July 1888, 8; *Argus*, 2 August 1888, 9. The Joadja Cup is probably the oldest extant soccer trophy in Australia. The miners also won regularly at home and in Sydney, in the final of the Gardiner Cup in 1889, for example.
182 *Argus*, 12 June 1891, 3.
183 *Argus*, 26 June 1891, 6.
184 *Argus*, 30 May 1892, 10; A more contemporary description would be 'soccering'.
185 *Argus*, 27 June 1894, 3.
186 *Argus*, 16 July 1894, 6.
187 *Argus*, 13 August 1894, 6.
188 *Argus*, 6 August 1894, 6. For a game in decline the crowd, if accurate, is remarkable.
189 *Argus*, 15 August 1894, 6.
190 *Argus*, 1 September 1894, 5.
191 *Argus*, 3 September 1895, 7.

192 *Argus,* 11 March 1896, 7.

193 *Argus*, 22 June 1896, 6.

194 *West Australian, 9* July 1904, 8.

195 Grant (*Jack Pollard's Soccer Records*, n.d.) has him being transferred to New Zealand in 1890, 114. He names him as A A Gibb.

196 *Northern Star*, 8 July 1911, 9. Dr Opie was also involved in VFL football via the University Club in Melbourne. He was called to give evidence about two University players accused of match-fixing in 1908 (*Argus*, 18 June 1908, 6).

197 *Daily News*, 22 May 1896, 3.

198 Mosely, 'Soccer', 386.

199 Kreider, *The Soccerites*, 30.

200 *West Australian*, 7 May 1896, 3.

201 Kreider, *The Soccerites*, 30.

202 *Daily News,* 30 June 1900, 2.

203 *Inquirer & Commercial News*, 12 April 1901, 2.

204 *Albany Advertiser*, 13 September 1901, 4.

205 *West Australian*, 26 April 1902, 8.

206 Barker discusses this code tension and the strategies adopted by Australian Rules in fighting off soccer in 1905 (Barker, *Behind the Play*, 43).

207 *Daily News*, 2 June 1905, 8.

208 Cashman, *Sport in the National Imagination*, 166.

209 Hess et al., *A National Game*, 129.

210 *Daily News*, 20 November 1905, 3.

211 *Daily News*, 20 November 1905, 3.

212 Hess et al., *A National Game,* 188.

213 Hess et al., *A National Game*, 188.

214 *Advertiser*, 28 August 1908, 7.

215 *Age*, 28 August 1908, 10.

216 *Advertiser*, 28 August 1908, 7.

217 *Barrier Miner*, 13 May 1912, 3.

218 Hess et al., *A National Game,* 129–60.

219 *West Australian*, 21 April 1906, 12.

220 *West Australian*, 18 April 1908, 8.

221 *Daily News*, 2 May 1912, 2.

222 *West Australian,* 17 October 1914, 9.

223 Williams, *Marxism and Literature*, 128–35.

224 *Barrier Miner*, 1 July 1910, 7.

225 *Advertiser*, 7 June 1909, 9.

226 Kreider, *The Soccerites*, 88. The impending tour of the eastern states was noted briefly in the *Argus, 27* April 1909, 8.

227 *Advertiser,* 7 June 1909, 9.

228 Hay, 'Henry John Dockerty'.

229 *Argus*, 21 July 1908, p 7.

230 *Argus*, 25 July 1908, 17.

231 *Argus*, 10 August 1908, 5.

232 *Argus*, 15 August 1908, 16.

233 *Argus*, 12 September 1908, 7.

234 *Argus*, 3 October 1908, 17.

235 *Argus*, 15 July 1910, 4.

236 *Argus*, 19 September 1910, 5.

237 *Argus*, 18 July 1912, 4.

238 *Argus*, 14 July 1913, 12.

239 *Argus*, 14 July 1913, 12.

240 *Argus*, 6 October 1913, 5.

241  *Emerald Hill Record,* 9 May 1914, 3.

242  *Argus,* 29 June 1914, 7.

243  *Argus,* 29 June 1914, 7.

244  The *Winner,* 21 October 1914 claimed that soccer had 597 senior players.

245  *Sydney Morning Herald,* 6 March 1912, 11.

246  *Worker,* 22 April 1911, 5.

247  *Worker,* 23 April 1898, 9.

248  *Western Mail,* 22 September 1900, 51.

249  Reeves, *Up from the Underworld,* 49–50. Reeves also (56) alludes to soccer's sustaining importance during the Depression in the 1930s.

250  *Gippslander and Mirboo Times,* 27 August 1914, 3. The match report from a patriotic game in Mirboo North in support of the war effort in 1914 makes it clear that the playing groups were made up of immigrants loyal to Britain. It also suggests that the contest was a novel experience in the community. Interestingly, on account of one team failing to show because their employer refused to let them have time off, a group of 'Australians' stepped in and beat the Brits at their own game. Perhaps gripped by the ruling Victorian spirit of anti-soccerism, the reporter felt the need to comment: 'If the exhibition as seen on Saturday was a fair sample of soccer, all we can say is the game cannot-be compared with the Australian game of football' shortly before admitting somewhat contradictorily that 'the exhibition on Saturday was not one that the game should be judged on'.

251  *Brisbane Courier,* 26 June 1911, 7.

252  *Brisbane Courier,* 26 June 1911, 7.

253  This is the kind of local digging that needs to be done in the next generation. Local, undigitised sources will be used.

254  *Warwick Examiner and Times,* 1 June 1912, 1.

255  Future research might uncover more descriptive information about a game of 'English football' played in the town in 1861 (Warrnambool Football Netball Club, 'History of Warrnambool FC').

256  *Argus,* 3 June 1912, 10. Another Wallabies team played in the Adelaide senior competition. The result suggests that this was not the team in question.

257  *West Australian,* 5 June 1912, 9.

258  *Geraldton Guardian,* 11 June 1912, 2.

259  *Northern Star,* 14 July 1911, 8.

260  *Cumberland Argus,* 29 June 1912, 6.

261  *Cairns Post,* 6 July 1912, 5.

262  *Queanbeyan Age,* 23 July 1912, 2.

263  *Rockhampton Morning Bulletin,* 10 September 1912, 5.

264  *Warwick Examiner and Weekly Times,* 26 June 1912, 5.

265  *Brisbane Courier,* 29 July 1912, 5.

266  *Brisbane Courier,* 20 August 1912, 4.

267  *Warwick Examiner and Times,* 2 July 1913, 4.

268  *Warwick Examiner and Times,* 5 July 1913, 4.

269  *Warwick Examiner and Times,* 12 July 1913, 4.

270  *Warwick Examiner and Times,* 12 July 1913, 4.

271  *Warwick Examiner and Times,* 10 September 1913, 4.

272  *Warwick Examiner and Times,* 8 September 1913, 4.

273  *Courier-Mail,* 16 May 1936, 23.

274  Soccer revived once more in the Warwick region sometime after the Second World War. And as with so many soccer associations around Australia, those responsible began in a pioneering spirit, probably unaware that they were not the first to bring this game to this place.

     In 2012 it came as a surprise to many of those involved in soccer in Warwick that the year represented the 100th anniversary of the first stirrings of organised soccer in their region. They were under the impression that the game had never been played there until the 1950s or 1960s, and they were even unclear about that.

275 ANZAC stands for the Australia and New Zealand Army Corps and in Australian mythological terms often stands metonymically for the entirety of Australian military history. Moreover, the term is sometimes deployed as a symbol of 'Australian spirit' in general.

276 *Weekly Times*, 3 August 1918, 21.

277 Since 1995 Collingwood and Essendon have battled for AFL ANZAC supremacy at the MCG. St George and Eastern Suburbs commemorate the day in the NRL. In recent years a cross-Tasman NRL game between Melbourne Storm and New Zealand Warriors has also been added to the ANZAC Day mix. In 2013 AFL club St Kilda FC played their inaugural ANZAC Day game, in Wellington. Blackburn's *War, Sport and the ANZAC Tradition* is a good coverage of the field.

278 See Lake, Reynolds and McKenna, *What's Wrong With Anzac?* for a thoroughgoing history and critique of the rise of ANZAC Day in this period.

279 Green, 'Anzac Day is about their deaths, not our lives'. Green sees a great deal of transference involved in the sporting cooption of ANZAC: 'The deeds of our veterans are at once honoured and dragged down to the humdrum of ordinary life through constant acts of easy equivalence. The further we travel from those great wars that saw the mass involvement of ordinary men and women, the more we see their sacrifice, their often terrible sacrifice, as analogous to the recognisable struggles of our modern lives: the valor of footballers, something as universal and banal as "mateship" ' (Green, 'Anzac Day is about their deaths, not our lives').

280 Less than one per cent of Australia's fighting force was recruited via the Sportsmen's Battalions (Booth and Tatz, *One-Eyed*, 100).

281 Phillips, 'Sport, War and Gender Images', 81.

282 Blair, 'Beyond the metaphor'.

283 Blair, 'Beyond the metaphor'.

284 Blair, 'Beyond the metaphor'.

285 A term search for 'sport' limited to the First World War in the Australian War Memorial's website http://www.awm.gov.au/ obtained 691 hits, the vast majority being photographs.

286 *Euroa Advertiser*, 21 July 1916, 5; also: *Horsham Times*, 21 June 1916, 3; *Warrnambool Standard*, 29 July 1916, 8; *West Gippsland Gazette*, 25 July 1916, 4; *Traralgon Record*, 21 July 1916, 6; *Bairnsdale Advertiser and Tambo and Omeo Chronicle*, 22 July 1916, 6; *Prahran Telegraph*, 27 May 1916, 5; *Camperdown Chronicle*, 20 April 1916, 2; *Cumberland Argus and Fruitgrowers Advocate*, 16 May 1916, 3; *West Australian*, 3 October 1916, 8.

287 The recent digitisation of Australian newspaper archives has made the discovery and collation of this genre a relatively easy matter. Perhaps the long-standing historiographical prejudice against history from below and a healthy distrust of editorial practices during wartime have also militated against the widespread and systematic use of these letters.

288 *Register*, 16 June 1915, 7.

289 *Warwick Examiner and Times*, 12 February 1917, 1.

290 *Launceston Examiner*, 3 September 1915, 8.

291 *Emerald Hill Record*, 10 February 1917, 2.

292 *Emerald Hill Record*, 26 May 1917, 2.

293 *Emerald Hill Record*, 15 September 1917, 2.

294 *Emerald Hill Record*, 8 June 1918, 30.

295 *Emerald Hill Record*, 23 February 1918, 2.

296 *Emerald Hill Record*, 29 June 1918, 2.

297 *Emerald Hill Record*, 17 November 1917, 2.

298 *Emerald Hill Record*, 16 March 1918, 2.

299 *Emerald Hill Record*, 15 January 1916, 2.

300 See, for example, the *Football Record* 8, 4 June 1928, 3. This edition contained the following statement from 'Chatterer': 'Australia's game is recognised by people from other lands who have followed the codes of those countries as the most spectacular of any winter game of the kind, and the Soccer and Rugger lads who have settled among us and have taken to Aussie's football will tell you that it is the best of all'.

301 *Emerald Hill Record*, 5 February 1916, 3.

302 *Queenslander*, 22 April 1916, 18.

303 *Euroa Advertiser*, 19 May 1916, 3.

304 *Barrier Miner*, 31 December 1916, 2.

305 *Euroa Advertiser*, 19 March 1915, 3.

306 *Barrier Miner*, 7 February 1915, 1.

307 *Gippsland Times*, 27 September 1915, 2.

308 A player listed as B. Anderson played for the Moonyoonooka soccer team in 1914 (*Geraldton Guardian*, 21 May 1914, 3).

309 Probably the newspaper's parenthesis.

310 *Geraldton Guardian*, 7 March 1916. 4.

311 *Nepean Times*, 27 May 1916, 6.

312 *Daily News*, 15 January 1917, 2.

313 *West Australian*, 20 May 1916, 9.

314 Research so far suggests that the soccer-dominant letters seem to come mainly from WA, with some from Queensland and NSW. Soccer subdominant is very much the tonality from Victoria. Further work needs to be done to establish patterns and emphases.

315 Andrews, *The Anzac Illusion*, 44.

316 Bean, *Official History of Australia in the War of 1914–1918*.

317 Bean, *Official History of Australia in the War of 1914–1918*.

318 These figures are drawn from the 'First to Fall' website http://www.anzacsite.gov.au/1landing/first-to-fall/11battalion/index.html. The remainder were made up of English-born (14) and Scots-born (6) and 2 Irishmen, 1 Englishman born in Brazil, 1 Maltese and 1 man whose parents were domiciled in India. All those without a given place of birth and with next of kin domiciled in Australia have been attributed Australia-born status.

319 Williamson, *Soccer Anzacs*, vii. It is not clear whether the Geraldton numbers are included in this figure.

320 *Daily News*, 3 April 1915, 8.

321 *West Australian*, 16 October 1915, 9. These figures were by no means accurate or up to date at the time. The Caledonian figure is clearly incomplete, given their tragic story.

322 *Geraldton Guardian*, 14 June 1919, 4.

323 *Geraldton Guardian and Express*, 3 June 1933, 4.

324 Dockerty claimed in February 1915 that 'his organisation, numbered 500 members, and 200 had already gone to the front' (*Barrier Miner*, 13 February 1915, 6). In July, after the Gallipoli campaign began, it was claimed by another representative that 'they had a total of 170 out of 550 players (30 per cent) serving with the colors or out at Broadmeadows' (*Malvern Standard*, 3 July 1915, 6). The claim in the *Winner* was made on 21 October 1914.

325 *Argus*, 23 June 1919, 9.

326 Ian Syson and Athas Zafiris researched this matter. Unfortunately, all Association records from the period have long since disappeared. (One of the few existing remnants of the period is the Dockerty Cup itself, along with some team photographs.) The quandary was how to confirm or rebut the claimed figures, which were: (a) between 500 and 600 players in Victoria; (b) 150–200 enlistments before the end of 1915; and (c) around 300 further enlistments throughout the war.

Every soccer article (mostly match reports) in the *Argus* and the *Winner* in 1914 and 1915 was read. The names of players and their teams were extracted where possible. Each report listed the goalscorers and the better players as well as noting injuries and other matters. Lists of players were found but only occasionally.

The data collected therefore is necessarily incomplete. Players who never scored and never shone remain largely invisible. Rarely are first names given, though first initials are sometimes included. Moreover, spelling of surnames seemed not to be a major priority for reporters. Even star players, like the Northumberland and Durhams goalkeeper Robison/Robinson, were subject to misnaming. One final irritation was the fact that own goals were represented as being scored by the player who scored but were not registered in the list of scorers as an own goal. If we were not careful a player could be named in the wrong club.

The research process benefitted from the discovery of 'motherload' documents. The first was published on 28 April 1915, soon after Gallipoli but too soon to represent a response to that event. The *Winner* released a list of the names and clubs of 143 enlisted players. The second vital list was the 1919 *Age* publication of the names of the 34 Melbourne Thistle players who enlisted and the eight of that number who perished in the war.

From these sources and within the limitations outlined above the researchers expected to uncover the names of perhaps 80 per cent of Victorian soccer players in the years 1914–1915, so they were confident of getting around 400 player names.

Using an admittedly incomplete net, more than 500 names of Melbourne senior soccer players were gathered. Additional to these are 22 referees and the 150 non-metropolitan players discovered in places like Mildura, Geelong and Kyabram. To this figure needs to be added the 40 or more Wonthaggi players yet to be identified and named.

Other tangential findings include that Melbourne soccer players were mostly of Church of England or Presbyterian faiths while Catholics represented a 10 per cent minority against their national proportion of over 20%; and very few soccer players were from the professions, most being skilled tradesman or labourers.

327  *Emerald Hill Record*, 24 April 1915, 3.
328  *Emerald Hill Record*, 17 July 1915, 4.
329  *Mercury,* 19 August 1921, 4.
330  *Mercury*, 31 March 1915, 5.
331  *Examiner,* 1 April 1915, 6.
332  *Register*, 1 April 1915, 10.
333  *Brisbane Courier*, 4 April 1919, 11.
334  *Cumberland Argus and Fruitgrowers Advocate*, 15 September 1917, 10.
335  'World War 1: Gallipoli Campaign 4/4'. See the image at 5.49–5.52 in this video at http://www.youtube.com/watch?v=SQsCQ4k8WTA.
336  Australian War Memorial, https://www.awm.gov.au/collection/C1001488/ (accessed 16/5/18).
337  *Geelong Advertiser*, 12 November 1915, 2.
338  Adelaide *Register*, 10 August 1923, 7.
339  *Sydney Morning Herald*, 3 July 1936, 16.
340  Sydney *Sun-Herald*, 6 September, 1954, 41.
341  Cashman, *Sport in the National Imagination*, 109.
342  *West Australian*, 22 May 1915, 9.
343  *Brisbane Courier*, 4 April 1919, 11.
344  Williamson, *Soccer Anzacs*, 113.
345  Hay and Syson, *The Story of Football in Victoria*, 10–11.
346  This 'boom' is discussed in depth by John Kallinikios, *Soccer Boom*.
347  *Mercury*, 3 April 1931, 8. The name 'Derwentside' is derived from the Derwent, Hobart's main river.
348  These issues are canvassed by Hay in 'Our Wicked Foreign Game'.
349  'Dinkum' means 'authentic' in Australian slang. A 'Dinkum Aussie' is an authentic Australian.
350  *Sunshine Advocate*, 5 November 1927, 1. This letter is so extreme that it is possible that it was a hoax – what might be called trolling today.
351  English schoolteachers were seen as especially proactive in illicitly introducing soccer to Australian schoolboys. Prior to the war this tension came to a head in Perth, WA. A retrospective on the death of J J Simons, the founder of the Young Australian [Football] League, mentions this attitude in relation to 1905: 'Soccer was firmly established in the schools, but Mr Simons fought for the national game until he had overcome the prejudices of English schoolteachers' (*Daily News*, 25 October 1948, 6).
352  These issues are discussed in Chapter 3.
353  *Argus*, 9 August 1920, 4.
354  *Argus*, 26 July 1920, 5; *Argus*, 23 July 1920, 4.
355  The 1927 ANZAC Day game at Moonee Valley (*Argus,* 9 April 1927, 25).
356  Hay, ' "Our Wicked Foreign Game" ', 165–86.

357 *Football Record*, 26 May 1920, 19.

358 The Amateur Sports Ground was the name given to an area of land in what is presently known as the Sports Precinct in Melbourne. It has never fully settled into a long-term function. It became the Motordrome in the 1920s, hosting motor racing, Australian Rules and soccer matches. Redeveloped as Olympic Park for the 1956 Olympics, it became the home of Melbourne soccer for more than 50 years before being demolished to make a training ground for Collingwood [Australian Rules] FC.

359 *Argus*, 28 June 1924, 19. The Public Service Football Club applied in 1924 to enter the VFL in the following season.

360 Perhaps the lukewarm relationship between the VFL and VFA (never smooth and often at odds) has some bearing on the fact that soccer was not excluded from the ground in this instance. Soccer was played there from the mid-1920s and a lease was obtained by the Victorian Soccer Association in April 1928.

361 This game was eventually relegated to 'B' international status by the FA. Subsequent references to this game will be to the 'Test'.

362 *Football Record*, 23 May 1925, 19–20.

363 *Argus*, 20 May 1925, 24.

364 *Argus*, 23 May 1925, 19.

365 *Argus*, 23 May 1925, 19.

366 This fact is at odds with the assumption that spectators would be strangers to the game.

367 On the face of it the attendance was only on a par with the two least-attended VFL games held on the day and was shaded even by Melbourne v North Melbourne the following week.

368 *Argus*, 25 May 1925, 6.

369 A Chinese tour provided an earlier example of the game's earning power elsewhere in Australia. In 1923 nearly 50,000 attended the Sydney Cricket Ground, and 26,000 in Adelaide. Total takings on the NSW and Queensland legs of the tour were nearly £8000. For comments on the 'immensely successful' English tour, see *Sporting Globe*, 25 July 1925, 4.

370 *Argus*, 14 August 1911, 4.

371 *Queensland Times*, 17 August 1912, 8

372 In September 1923 the Cricket Club reported that 'soccer football' had brought the club £311 (£72 nett) from 4 days of ground use – slotted into weeks where FFC had the bye or no senior VFL football was played. This figure needs augmentation with whatever takings resulting from the attendance of 12,000 (possibly £300 at 6d per head) at the so-called Chinese game (the team was from Hong Kong) played after the figures were released. This can be contrasted with the earnings from VFL football of £4106 (around £1700 nett) from 8 days of senior football and 8 days of 2nds football (*Referee* 19 September 1923, 14).

373 *Argus*, 14 May 1927, 22.

374 *Argus*, 11 June 1927, 22.

375 In its history the Fitzroy Cricket Ground has hosted over 100 senior soccer matches, including one National Soccer League match in 1977, when Heidelberg beat Brisbane Lions 4–1, and some intense State League matches between Heidelberg and Hellas that attracted large crowds, one of which was over 14,000. Yet this rich aspect of the ground's history has been largely forgotten, especially by those who might be expected to remember. See for example, Marc Fiddian's *Forever Fitzroy: A History of the Brunswick St Oval*. This brief history of sport on the ground covers cricket, baseball and Australian Rules, but it would seem from Fiddian's perspective that soccer is a game that never happened on the Fitzroy Cricket Ground. *Age* also reported on 2 July that the wrong admission charge had been advertised at three shillings instead of one. This may have had some limiting effect on the crowd.

376 See Hay and Syson, *The Story of Football in Victoria*, 9–10.

377 Hay and Murray. *A History of Football in Australia*, 178.

378 It is hard to imagine a comparative piece of writing being published today, especially in an edition designed to showcase the merits of the game.

379 See the Epilogue. Dyer claimed in the Melbourne press that soccer was such a soft and unskillful game that he could gather together a team of VFL players that would beat the Dockerty Cup champions, Slavia, at soccer. His team was beaten 8–0 in a 50-minute match.

380 If the author is referring to a game he saw Newcastle United play (possibly their first home game on 1 September, when they were beaten 5–2 by Brentford), he really needed to point out their Second-Division status. He might also have added that the club was in a shambles, having been relegated the previous season and only just avoiding relegation in 1934–35 on goal average. As he rightly pointed out, they weren't very good! The Sunderland crowd figure was obtained from 11v11.com http://www.11v11.com/matches/sunderland-v-huddersfield-town-25-august-1934-67316/ (accessed 16/5/18).

381 Mosely and Murray, 'Soccer', 214.

382 Hay, '"Our Wicked Foreign Game"', 172.

383 This is not a uniquely Australian experience. In *The Far Corner* Pearson writes about the same 'disappearance' in north-east England.

384 Hay has focused on the phrase 'Our wicked foreign game' (2006, 180 ). He notes it was quoted by VJM Dixon, editor of *Soccer News*, in his editorial of 24 July 1954, 2. Dixon was writing about the forthcoming tour of a New Zealand team to Victoria: 'The usual panic is on in the home of another code [Australian Rules Football] and all clubs are combining to make sure "Our Wicked Foreign Game" shall not use any of their hallowed ovals'. He went on to say that the difficulty had been overcome and a suitable venue arranged. Brunswick Oval, home of the Fitzroy Cricket Club and the Fitzroy Football Club ground, was to be used on 11 and 14 August 1954 for games against Victoria and Australia respectively (*Soccer News*, 31 July 1954, 7 & 10).

385 Hope, 'Australia', 1972, 190.

386 Paul Mavroudis argues that soccer is often figured in Australian literature as foreign or as being in opposition to local games. Australian literature when it does refer to soccer contains many 'reminders of the game's foreign status and its lack of importance in Australia' (Mavroudis, 'Against the Run of Play', 492).

387 Dawe, 'Life cycle'.

388 Maynard, *The Aboriginal Soccer Tribe* is a very recent exception. See also Syson, 'An Absence of Option'.

389 Kallinikios, *Soccer Boom*.

390 In 1952 'the VFL directed its operatives to secure all available public sporting space in Melbourne in order to stifle the burgeoning threat posed by soccer's migrant-inspired growth. Similar moves had been made in 1927 and 1928 when British migrants so rattled the VFL that it wrote "with alarm" of this "foreign code". The 1950s boom in migration promised to be far more of a problem than that of the 1920s. In 1958 a Melbourne soccer club sought to lease a council ground usually used by an Australian Rules club. In response to the application one rules-supporting sneered "let them play . . . in the gutter". Melbourne's reputation for paranoia was crowned in 1965 when youths daubed anti-soccer slogans over Middle Park, chopped down the goalposts and tried to set fire to the grandstand' (Mosely, *Soccer in New South Wales*, 271.)

391 'Footy takes on the soccer boys', *Sporting Globe*, 14 November 1964, 15.

392 Barotajs, 'Slavia were surprised', *Truth*, 21 November 1964. It is ironic that the typical sexist attitudes of the time are now turned on their heads by the way in which soccer and Australian Rules today are competing to attract women players as part of their development strategies (see Barr, 'Slavia won match 8–0', *Age*, 16 November 1964).

393 Personal interview conducted on 29 June 2009. All subsequent references to McMeechan are from this interview.

394 Dyer, *Truth*, 21 November 1964.

# INDEX